Advance Praise for *Tiny Engines of Abundance*

"This book demonstrates the fallacy of 200 years of proclaiming the necessity of industrial agriculture to feed the world. As well as using case studies from around the world to show the efficiency of peasant productivity, it also shows the various ways peasant livelihoods have been obstructed, attacked, and betrayed. The author debunks the arguments used to justify those attacks, which continue today, namely that peasant contributions are too low for economies built on incessant expansion and accumulation. This book is essential reading for anyone interested in food sovereignty, which should be all of us."

—Miguel A. Altieri, emeritus professor of agroecology, University of California at Berkeley, and founder and past president of the Latin American Scientific Society for Agroecology (SOCLA).

T0277149

Tiny Engines
of Abundance

ALSO IN THE CRITICAL DEVELOPMENT STUDIES SERIES

COVID-19 and the Future of Capitalism: Postcapitalist Horizons Beyond Neo-Liberalism (2021)
by Efe Can Gürcan, Ömer Ersin Kahraman & Selen Yanmaz

Extractivism: Politics, Economy and Ecology (2021)
by Eduardo Gudynas

The Political Economy of Agrarian Extractivism: Lessons from Bolivia (2020)
by Ben M. McKay

Development in Latin America: Toward a New Future (2019)
by Maristella Svampa, translation by Mark Rushton

Politics Rules: Power, Globalization and Development (2019)
by Adam Sneyd

Critical Development Studies: An Introduction (2018)
by Henry Veltmeyer & Raúl Delgado Wise

Tiny Engines
of Abundance

A History of Peasant
Productivity and Repression

JIM HANDY

CRITICAL DEVELOPMENT STUDIES

Copyediting: Jane Butler
Cover Painting: Pedro Rafael González Chavajay
Design: John van der Woude, JVDW Designs
Printed and bound in Canada

Published in North America by Fernwood Publishing
32 Oceanvista Lane, Black Point, Nova Scotia, B0J 1B0
and 748 Broadway Avenue, Winnipeg, Manitoba, R3G 0X3
www.fernwoodpublishing.ca

Published in the rest of the world by Practical Action Publishing
27a Albert Street, Rugby, Warwickshire CV21 2SG, UK

Fernwood Publishing Company Limited gratefully acknowledges the financial support
of the Government of Canada through the Canada Book Fund and the Canada Council
for the Arts, the Nova Scotia Department of Communities, Culture and Heritage, the
Manitoba Department of Culture, Heritage and Tourism under the Manitoba
Publishers Marketing Assistance Program and the Province of Manitoba, through
the Book Publishing Tax Credit, for our publishing program.

Library and Archives Canada Cataloguing in Publication

Title: Tiny engines of abundance: a history of peasant productivity and repression
/ by Jim Handy.
Names: Handy, Jim, 1952- author.
Series: Critical development studies.
Description: Series statement: Critical development studies |
Includes bibliographical references and index.
Identifiers: Canadiana (print) 20210353929 | Canadiana (ebook) 20210363207 |
ISBN 9781773635217 (softcover) | ISBN 9781773635439 (EPUB) |
ISBN 9781773635446 (PDF)
Subjects: LCSH: Peasants—History. | LCSH: Sustainable agriculture—History.
Classification: LCC HD1521 .H36 2022 | DDC 305.5/633—dc23

Contents

Critical Development Studies Series

Three decades of uneven capitalist development and neoliberal globalization have devastated the economies, societies, livelihoods and lives of people around the world, especially those in societies of the Global South. Now more than ever, there is a need for a more critical, proactive approach to the study of global and development studies. The challenge of advancing and disseminating such an approach — to provide global and development studies with a critical edge — is on the agenda of scholars and activists from across Canada and the world and those who share the concern and interest in effecting progressive change for a better world.

This series provides a forum for the publication of small books in the interdisciplinary field of critical development studies — to generate knowledge and ideas about transformative change and alternative development. The editors of the series welcome the submission of original manuscripts that focus on issues of concern to the growing worldwide community of activist scholars in this field. Critical development studies (CDS) encompasses a broad array of issues ranging from the sustainability of the environment and livelihoods, the political economy and sociology of social inequality, alternative models of local and community-based development, the land and resource-grabbing dynamics of extractive capital, the subnational and global dynamics of political and economic power, and the forces of social change and resistance, as well as the contours of contemporary struggles against the destructive operations and ravages of capitalism and imperialism in the twenty-first century.

The books in the series are designed to be accessible to an activist readership as well as the academic community. The intent is to publish a series of small books (54,000 words, including bibliography, endnotes, index and front matter) on some of the biggest issues in the interdisciplinary field of critical development studies. To this end, activist scholars from across the world in the field of development studies and related academic disciplines are invited to submit a proposal or the draft of a book that conforms to the stated aim of the series. The editors will consider the submission of complete manuscripts within the 54,000-word limit. Potential authors are encouraged to submit a proposal that includes a rationale and short synopsis of the book, an outline of proposed chapters, one or two sample chapters, and a brief biography of the author(s).

Series Editors

HENRY VELTMEYER is a research professor at Universidad Autónoma de Zacatecas (Mexico) and professor emeritus of International Development Studies at Saint Mary's University (Canada), with a specialized interest in Latin American development. He is also co-chair of the Critical Development Studies Network and a co-editor of Fernwood's Agrarian Change and Peasant Studies series. The CDS Handbook: Tools for Change (Fernwood, 2011) was published in French by University of Ottawa Press as Des outils pour le changement : Une approche critique en études du développement and in Spanish as Herramientas para el Cambio, with funding from Oxfam UK by CIDES, Universidad Mayor de San Andrés, La Paz, Bolivia.

ANNETTE AURÉLIE DESMARAIS is the Canada Research Chair in Human Rights, Social Justice and Food Sovereignty at the University of Manitoba (Canada). She is the author of La Vía Campesina: Globalization and the Power of Peasants (Fernwood, 2007), which has been republished in French, Spanish, Korean, Italian and Portuguese, and Frontline Farmers: How the National Farmers Union Resists Agribusiness and Creates our New Food Future (Fernwood, 2019). She is co-editor of Food Sovereignty: Reconnecting Food, Nature and Community (Fernwood, 2010); Food Sovereignty in Canada: Creating Just and Sustainable Food Systems (Fernwood, 2011); and Public Policies for Food Sovereignty: Social Movements and the State (Routledge, 2017).

RAÚL DELGADO WISE is a research professor and director of the PhD program in Development Studies at the Universidad Autónoma de Zacatecas (Mexico). He holds the prestigious UNESCO Chair on Migration and Development and is executive director of the International Migration and Development Network, as well as author and editor of some twenty books and more than a hundred essays. He is a member of the Mexican Academy of Sciences and editor of the book series, Latin America and the New World Order, for Miguel Angel Porrúa publishers and chief editor of the journal *Migración y Desarrollo*. He is also a member of the international working group, People's Global Action on Migration Development and Human Rights.

1 "Swept Away through Injustice"

I live in the prairies, the heartland of Canadian industrial agriculture, and I teach at the University of Saskatchewan. The University's College of Agriculture, one of Canada's largest, is dedicated to "improving" large-scale industrial agriculture. We are regularly warned by our College colleagues that these improvements are necessary to feed our hungry planet. Support for large-scale industrial agriculture is thus framed as a moral requirement; to do otherwise would supposedly condemn millions around the world to food scarcity, hunger and starvation. I am a bit surprised the College doesn't have a large portrait of Thomas Robert Malthus hanging in its atrium. This kind of perceived moral obligation is an important part of what the University of Saskatchewan self-righteously declares is its mission: to be "the university the world needs."

I was recently reminded of exactly what such support for industrial, large-scale agriculture means. On July 5, 2021, in the immediate aftermath of the most extreme heat wave ever to hit parts of western Canada (and western United States), I was sent a rather disturbing video that advertised land for rent from Saskatchewan's largest landowner. Robert Andjelic has built an empire of more than 218,000 acres of land in the province. The video was pitching a parcel of 22,000 acres for rent. A talking head explained that improvements to this piece of land were so recent they did not show up on Google satellite imagery. The video provided its own images. Where there had been landscape broken by the occasional stand of trees, some windbreaks and hedges, some sloughs and wetlands, and a few small hills, the company spokesperson explained, the land had been changed. The trees were gone, the windbreaks removed, and as the spokesperson enthusiastically proclaimed, the sloughs had been drained so that the land could now be farmed "from corner to corner." It was one big industrial agricultural landscape.

I had multiple concerns on viewing this video. There is little doubt that

Andjelic's company felt that the boasted millions of dollars spent on improvements would appeal to those seeking to rent land in the industrialized agricultural spirit of the age, notwithstanding the disappearance of wetlands and the grave reality of climate change, not in the distant future but now.

Along with a certain horror at the environmental monstrosity this represented, the video also prompted a vague feeling of déjà vu. It called to mind other accounts from earlier periods of agricultural improvement. Those promoting agricultural improvement often touted the benefits of clearing the land, the value of bigness and the supposed miracles created by the expenditure of capital on the land. Others, however, detailed the damage done through such actions and offered alternatives in the form of small-scale, peasant[1] agriculture.

In England in 1798, Sir Thomas Bernard, a wealthy member of the English gentry, sent a note to the Board of Agriculture and Internal Improvement. Bernard was the owner of a large estate and a member of the Board, a semi-public organization meant to represent the interests of large estate owners and promote agricultural "improvement." Bernard, however, was one of a small group of owners of large estates who expressed concern about the direction of agricultural change. He was especially worried about increasing poverty among rural workers who were deprived of the small bits of land they could farm independently. He described a very small farm near Tadcaster he had often admired when passing on the road. One day he stopped to inquire. According to Bernard's note, the farm was rented by an old man named Britton Abbot. It consisted of a cottage and a *rood* of land (a quarter of an acre or a tenth of a hectare), "inclosed by a ... hedge; and containing the cottage, fifteen apple trees, one green gage, and three winesour plum trees, two apricot-trees, several gooseberry and currant bushes, abundance of common vegetables, and three hives of bees." According to Bernard, Abbot and his wife of forty-five years got forty bushels of potatoes from the quarter acre, raised seven children and "lived very happy together" on the land.[2]

A little over fifty years later, John Davy, Inspector General of British Army Hospitals in the Caribbean, described typical house gardens there:

> The culture of these small properties is remarkable ... The crops grown are extremely various, and the produce commonly large ... On one little property ... there may be seen growing side by side, or intermixed, almost all the different vegetables which are in request in the island,—the sugar-cane, yam, sweet potatoe, eddoe, cassava, ground nut, ... the cotton plant, ginger, arrow root and the aloe.

He mentioned that they all raised chickens and goats, and some even had a cow.[3]

More than a century later, geographer Gene Wilken provided this account of intense peasant farming in Central America. In what he described as "dooryard gardens," he said, "plots of no more than 0.1 ha may contain two dozen or more ... plants," each carefully calibrated to take up distinct spaces, from tall trees (mango, papaya) to medium-height trees (banana, peach, citrus) to crops of maize, beans, tomatoes, chili peppers, squash and an understory of herbs, all intertwined with useful vines. No wonder such small-scale peasant agriculture, using intensive labour, brought forth seemingly miraculous returns. Wilken summarized this by suggesting, "any lingering images of the lazy, dull, noneconomic peasant farmer must surely have vanished."[4]

I could go on with this list (and will in the chapters that follow). Taken together, these accounts provide over 200 years of descriptions of the marvellous productivity of small-scale, peasant agriculture. Sometimes sympathetic, often astonished, observers noted what should have been obvious to anyone seriously considering the nature of agricultural production: the return from any piece of land is directly proportionate to the amount of labour and care that goes into it. Almost all these observers described an agriculture that was startling in its diversity, yet remarkably similar in many respects. Around the world, throughout history, those with control over tiny plots of land converted them into gardens. Crops not only used up all available space on the ground but grew to different heights, with roots that tapped the soil at varying depths. Different plants replenished the soil, fixing nitrogen or providing an abundance of organic litter. Others provided shade, protected more fragile crops from wind or had roots that were especially important in binding the soil and preventing erosion. Some plants did better in particularly damp soils, others flourished in dry, sandy or rich soils. Some produced early, providing nutrition before the full harvest came, others bore fruit late, extending the harvest and allowing labour demands to be spread out. Getting the right mix required years of experience, hard work and constant care. As one Guatemalan reformer proclaimed, the land had to be worked with a combination of the "hoe and love."[5] The right mix also required careful experimentation. These accounts describe a remarkable array of "new" crops, borrowed from far-flung parts of the world. It was peasant producers who insured that a broad range of new world crops, from potatoes to tomatoes to corn, became staples of small-scale production — from Europe to China and in between.

The lives depicted here might be surprising to some. We have been programmed, through 200 years of writing about improvement, progress, agricultural modernization and development — 200 years of proclaiming the moral imperative of improved industrial agriculture to feed the world — to conflate "peasant" with poverty. We have been programmed to regard a peasant existence as synonymous with "almost idiotic wretchedness," as one description of Irish cottiers suggested in the 1830s.[6] It could be wretched in times of particular stress, such as crop failure, or more often, repression and dispossession. Peasant livelihoods should not be romanticized. There is a reason commentators often saw these lives as miserable, poverty-stricken and without hope. As one Japanese doctor suggested in the 1920s, "There is no one as miserable as a peasant."[7] As anyone who has sought to feed a family from a sizeable garden can imagine, peasant lives were often full of deprivation and despair. Relationships in peasant communities could be acrimonious; conflict over land abounded, between neighbours, between sexes and across generations. Young people often took the least opportunity to flee the confines of their peasant communities and embrace both the freedoms and the potential in bigger centres or in distant lands. More often, though, descriptions of peasant livelihoods speak of determined self-reliance, carefully limited needs, simple comforts and hard-won independence. Peasant livelihoods often were (and are) pieced together with equal mixes of hard work, ingenuity and anxiety. In many regions, such self-reliance is, perhaps ironically, also dependent on the support of the community, the embrace of shared space and culture as much as a convenience of interests that counsel co-operation. What often emerges in these descriptions of peasant livelihoods is not wretchedness but abundance.

The three descriptions provided above were meant as advertisements, as surely as Andjelic's soaring description of his newly created environmental catastrophe was meant as an enticement to tenants. They were designed to defend peasants from attacks and policies that threatened them. They were also meant as counterweights to an onslaught of arguments that sought to justify taking these tiny plots of land away from those who had worked them so carefully. Bernard explained how Abbot had similarly lost a piece of land he had carefully cultivated when it had been included in an enclosure some years earlier. With the seizure of his land, "when he had six young children … and his wife preparing to lie in of a seventh, his whole little system of economy and arrangement was at once destroyed; his house, his garden, his little field taken from him."[8] Bernard hoped that his account of Abbot's steady productivity might help turn aside measures that were increasing rural poverty in the name of agricultural improvement everywhere he looked. Davy's account was meant to help blunt actions designed to force recently liberated ex-slaves from their holdings and back to labour on sugar. Wilken's was partly an appeal to better consider peasant agriculture in the midst of policy and legislation favouring the expansion of agro-export plantations. The fact that for 200 years these carefully weighed but glowing descriptions of peasant agriculture were considered necessary tells us much about the persistence of arguments to the contrary. Indeed, attacks on peasants, both physical, in the form of repression and dispossession, and intellectual, in the form of arguments about peasants being inimical to modernity and progress, may be one of history's most enduring attributes. As the Old Testament told readers more than 2000 years ago, "The field of the poor may yield much food, but it is swept away through injustice."[9] Scarcely a year has gone by since, it seems, that peasants have not been similarly repressed or attacked, most obviously because others more powerful or ruthless wanted their land and/or their labour. Very often this was linked to making peasants more dependent on wage labour, to allow their labour to be captured more easily by capital. As Marx described it, they became "sellers of themselves only after they had been robbed of all their own means of production."[10]

The justifications for such policies have grown more sophisticated over time: peasants were incompatible with progress, their "clumsy" labours, as the *Economist* described them,[11] could never be as productive as they would be under the direction of capital. They were threatening in a whole host of ways: prone to rebel and to have too many children, resistant to the embrace of the state or the nation, immune to the siren song of development. Despite careful stewardship of tiny plots of land that nurtured generations, peasants have been portrayed as serious threats to the environment, too slow to adapt and too quick to take offence.

Most consistently, it seems, peasants have been portrayed as incompatible with economic development. If, as Malthus tried to argue, "It is unquestionably true that wealth produces wants; but it is a still more important truth, that wants produce wealth,"[12] then peasants — with carefully limited needs, calibrated to returns from the land and adhered to as a means of insuring self-reliance and independence — have been for most of these 200 years anathema to both capitalists and development specialists. When, belatedly, some development programs and states embraced smallholder production, most often they ignored the careful rhythms of labour and the intricate use of land in often fragile locations. Instead, they sought to impose new crops, new agricultural techniques and new inputs that were often toxic and expensive. These new impositions threatened peasant livelihoods as surely as repression and dispossession.

This book provides a history of these tiny engines of abundance. It focuses on five regions at different times: England in the late 1700s and early 1800s, in the midst of what has often been called an agriculture revolution; Jamaica in the decades following slave emancipation in the 1830s; Guatemala in the middle of the 20th century as various governments sought to "modernize" Mayan *milpa* agriculture and eventually unleashed a genocide directed at both Mayan peasants and *milpa* agriculture; Nigeria in the 1960s and 1970s, when governments, advised by development specialists, sought to "capture" peasant production and boost export agriculture; and the Indian state of Kerala beginning in 1969, when important reforms helped nurture a much-admired "model" of development, one that has been threatened partly because an embrace of green revolution technology altered peasant hut-dweller production.

This is history and thus both describes these scenes of peasant productivity at particular moments in time and analyzes the sources, many of which need to be read against the grain, which provide us with these images. But this is also a history in its truest sense, replete, I hope, with lessons to help us understand and contend with contemporary problems.

These stories provide us with portraits of carefully limited needs, of sustainable livelihoods and of resilient independence attacked relentlessly and mercilessly in the name of capital, progress, development, modernity and/or the state. For 200 years, we were told that the key to economic growth was capital's ability to command labour; as the *Economist* newspaper said in 1844, "A pursuit ... for which the capitalist cannot pay wages should be instantly abandoned."[13] Peasants resisted that command.

Peasants were never against producing for the market, never opposed to experimentation and often quite prepared to work away from their gardens if the labour demands of their smallholdings permitted it. Most often, however, peasants balanced increased production with risk and tempered returns from the market with subsistence needs. As the French historian Fernand Braudel once noted about an earlier time, for capitalism to have unchallenged dominance, peasants needed to be "suppressed, at least contained and outmaneuvered," but such capitalist dreams were often stymied because peasants ensured "that one could not simply walk into the countryside and do as one pleased."[14] Peasants have never been opposed to the market, perceived as a place to exchange produce for income. Rather, they opposed capitalism if it meant capitalists could do what they wished in the peasants' countryside. For more than 200 years, those proposing "improvement" or "progress" or "development," have argued that to better peasant lives, "progress" meant denying them that for which they most yearned: some land of their own to farm and a cottage in which to live and raise their family. Most often peasants have disturbed the dreams of others: capitalists' yearnings for quiescent labourers at their beck and call, state planners' visions of orderly and ordered rural societies, development planners' schemes for economic growth that ignored peasants' visions of a good life. Perhaps it is time "development" paid attention to what peasants say they want.[15]

What about the constant apocalyptic pronouncements warning us that a deeper level of industrialized agriculture is necessary to feed the world, to save it from the "domestic imprudence" of peasants? Despite 200 years of attack, peasants and smallholders still produce most of the world's food. Despite 200 years of attack, they most often do this in sustainable ways that shepherd the land. Despite 200 years of attack, they still use the scarce resources (land, water and fertile soil) more efficiently than any other form of farming. And they do so by applying more of the most abundant of all factors of production: labour. Despite 200 years of attack, they might be our best source for healthy foods, societies and environments. Despite 200 years of attack, many still cling resolutely to an alternative vision of the good life. It is the modest proposition of this book that if we are to embrace real development for the future, we need to capture some of that vision. This would, this history suggests, foster stronger communities, deeper democracies and less wear and tear on a polluted, overheated and careworn world.

It is a bit rash for an author to suggest the emotions their writing might evoke in readers. I can with more certitude describe the emotions that reading these accounts and writing this book provoked in me. I first experienced a sense of awe at the wondrous productivity of these tiny engines of abundance — productivity described by commentator after commentator over the years, some initially intent on depicting peasant life as idiocy. I was awed at the industriousness and hard work that went into winning a peasant livelihood — again, industriousness described by commentator after commentator, some initially intent on demonstrating that peasants were indolent and lazy. And I was awed at the skill that turns making a living from tiny pieces of land into the art of peasant livelihood — again, often described by commentators initially intent on depicting peasants' wretchedness.

The other emotion that telling these stories evokes is anger at the lost opportunities and the unnecessary suffering that resulted from 200 years of attacks on peasant livelihoods. For 200 years we were told that peasants were inefficient and unproductive. For 200 years we were told peasants would have too many children and, thus, breed themselves out of existence or into misery if not curtailed. For 200 years we were told that peasants need to be dispossessed and displaced to allow for other "more efficient" uses of their labour, "supervised by capitalists," to enable economic growth and prosperity. For 200 years we have been told that hundreds of thousands — or millions or billions (pick your number) — of hungry mouths require that peasants be dispossessed to allow more industrious farmers to feed them. I hope this book helps make it clear how wrong we have been.

NOTES

1   Throughout this book, I use the term "peasant" in an inclusive manner, much as "campesino" is used in the Latin American literature. That is, I use it to refer to smallholders who farm land on which they make production decisions, produce both for subsistence and for the market and employ primarily family labour.

2   Sir Thomas Bernard, "An Account of a Cottage and Garden," *Annals of Agriculture, and Other Useful Arts* 30 (1798), 1–9.

3   John Davy, *The West Indies Before and Since Slave Emancipation*, London: W&F.G. Cash, 1854, 149–151.

4   Gene Wilken, *Good Farmers: Traditional Agricultural Resource Management in Mexico and Central America*, Berkeley: University of California Press, 1987, esp. 41, 49, 249, 250, 263.

5   Asamblea Constituyente, *Diario de sesiones: Asamblea constituyente de 1945*, Guatemala City: Tipografía Nacional, 1951, 751.

6   Cited in J. Killen et al., *The Famine Decade: Contemporary Accounts, 1841–1851*, Belfast: Blackstaff Press, 1995, 32.

7   Cited in M. Hane, *Peasants, Rebels, and Outcastes: The Underside of Modern Japan*, New York: Pantheon, 1982, 34–35.

8   Bernard, "An Account of a Cottage and Garden," *Annals* 30 (1798), 1–9.

9   Proverbs 13:23.

10   Karl Marx, *Capital, Vol. 1*, New York: International Publishers, 1967, 715.

11   *Economist*, "The Labourer's Panacea — The Allotment System," 2:62 (Nov. 2, 1844) 1369–1370.

12   T.R. Malthus, *Principles of Political Economy, Volume I*, (ed. John Pullen), Cambridge: Cambridge University Press, 1989, 470. [note: this is the 1820 edition, with edited changes for 1836 marked].

13   *Economist*, "The Labourer's Panacea — The Allotment System" 2:62 (Nov. 2, 1844) 1369–1370.

14   Fernand Braudel, *Civilization and Capitalism: 15th–18th Century, Vol 2: The Wheels of Commerce* (translated by Sîan Reynold), London: Collins, 1982, 251–253.

15   Part of the reluctance to foster development by providing peasants with what they want is related to perceptions of poverty and how best to "attack" it. For an account of an interesting and ultimately failed attempt to define the multiple and complicated dimensions of poverty — one that despite thousands of interviews with "poor" people was reduced to defining the poor as those who lived on less than $1.08 a day, see the World Bank's *World Development Report, 2000/2001*, 2001. For a discussion of the conflicts over the final draft of that report, see Robert Hunter Wade, "Making the World Development Report 2000: Attacking Poverty," *World Development* 29:8 (2001), 1435–1441.

2 "A Multiplication of Wretchedness" in England, 1750–1850

Thousands of people crowded into a public meeting held by the Royal Commission of Inquiry into widespread riots, often called the Rebecca Riots, in Wales in 1843. One poor soul said to the commissioners:

> Ah! They want to catch 'Becca and yet at the same time they do not know who she is; they are looking for 'Becca, they do not know where to find her, and yet she may be seen everywhere …. Who then is 'Becca? Everyone is 'Becca. She … thrives on our grievances … If you want to kill 'Becca, … give bread to the poor, and give them enough of it.[1]

This was neither the first nor the last of a long series of protests in rural England and Wales. Indeed, from the last few decades of the 18th until the middle of the 19th century, rural England was convulsed with unrest. There were food riots, opposition to the application of the Poor Laws, protests over rural wages and opposition to the enclosure of common lands. For more than half a century, rural life in England was so often punctuated by riots, protests and a notorious series of arson attacks that it is not much of an exaggeration to describe the situation as a rural war.

It was no secret that the cause of the unrest was the devastating and deepening level of rural poverty. In a letter sent to farmers near Stowmarket in Suffolk in 1844, the writer stated, "Gentlemen, I have thought it proper of wrighting these few words to show and let you know how pore are oppressed in this place … I ask what you must expect but fire."[2]

This chapter argues that appreciation for the productivity of very small-scale "peasant" producers would have alleviated a century of distress in rural

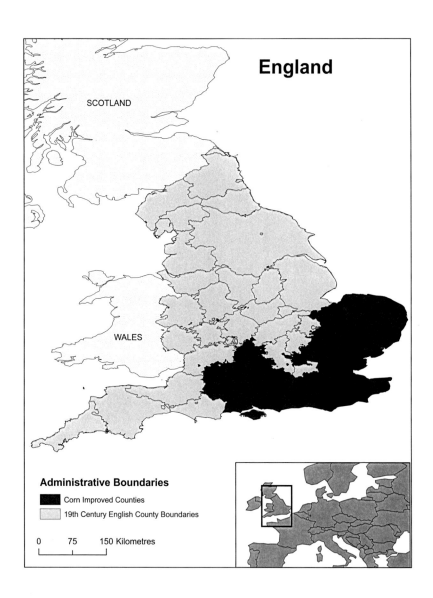

England

SCOTLAND

WALES

Administrative Boundaries

Corn Improved Counties

19th Century English County Boundaries

0   75   150 Kilometres

England and Wales. Important among the causes of increased poverty was the determination by landowners, farmers and the purveyors of "political economy" — newly masquerading as a science — to make the rural poor entirely dependent on wages. In doing so, they argued vehemently against any proposition that would give the poor access to land to farm independently. Fortunately for us, we have a range of testimonies — including Bernard's discussion of Brinton Abbot outlined in the previous chapter — that not only attests to the productivity of peasant farmers but also presents persuasive arguments about the social benefits to be derived from small-scale, cottage agriculture.[3] These testimonies had little effect in the march to chain labour and land to the demands of capital. Their limited effect was not because they didn't present persuasive arguments. Rather, the determination of large farmers to have labourers fully dependent on them and the political economists' constant refrains about the miracle of capital combined to drown out these expressions of concern. Multiple testimonies make it clear, however, that had England followed a different path, if the social and productive benefits of peasant agriculture had been abetted and tapped, the country would have produced more food for its hungry population and a hundred years of desperate poverty might have been avoided.

An Agricultural Revolution or Too Many People?

What were the sources of this increasing poverty and the resultant unrest? Some pointed to population increase. It is certainly true that the population of England and Wales increased dramatically in the period between 1750 and 1850, from just over six million people in 1751 to just under eighteen million a century later. Most famously, Thomas Robert Malthus declared in 1798 that rural poverty was a direct result of this population growth, spurred on, he argued, by the "attraction between the sexes" and the debilitating effects of too-easy poor relief. However, an examination of rural life in England and Wales in this century of calamity for the rural poor offers reasons other than population increase for deepening poverty.

If excess population was the cause of increasing poverty and hunger, a logical pursuit would have been to get the most food out of the available land. Instead, for a century, England pursued policies that sought to prevent those who would willingly work the land from having access to it. As we will see, England suffered from the bizarre but not infrequent combination of a hungry population, workers ready and able to work the land and good land sitting idle. One reason for this strange combination was the constant assertion that only capital could unlock the land's productive promise.

England experienced what has been described as an "agricultural revolution" during this century. There is substantial debate about exactly what was involved in this revolution and when it occurred. It is most often argued that a series of changes to both the *structure* of agriculture in England (enclosure of common lands; shorter, more commercial leases for larger farms to tenant farmers; the investment of significant amounts of capital in draining and fencing land) and the *practice* of agriculture (increased use of new root crops for animal feed, more stall-feeding animals, better cover for pasture, and increased use of both manure and imported fertilizer, which meant less land had to be kept fallow) led to dramatically improved yields. Despite significant debate among agricultural historians over the years, the assessment of a beneficial revolution in agricultural productivity during this period has been remarkably durable. In 1943, G.E. Fussell described the period as one of "improved agriculture of such industry that it is wonderful to relate."[4] More than fifty years later, Mark Overton still identified dramatic increases in productivity in this period, especially an "unprecedented" improvement in labour productivity in agriculture, as the major component in an agricultural revolution.[5]

This purported increase in agricultural productivity lent English agriculture an almost mythical status among agricultural historians, and even more importantly, among economists and others advising "poor" countries about economic development in the years after World War II. The English experience — in which, it is said, agricultural production not only kept up with population increase but freed large numbers to join the cheap labour force for industrialization — became the blueprint used by development economists in post-independence Africa and elsewhere.[6] By the 19th century, as agricultural "improvement" morphed into "high" agriculture and concentrated more fully on improved pasture, stall-feeding and manure, English agricultural efficiency was also touted as a rare example of a benign, sustainable large-scale agriculture system. E.A Wrigley has termed this "advanced organic agriculture."[7] For many, successfully replicating the English transition to industrial prosperity with the support of an efficient agricultural sector meant replicating rural English social structures marked by large-scale, capital-intensive farms and a rural labour force dependent on wages. Throughout this hundred-year period, it was considered most important to prevent the proliferation of small-scale, peasant agriculture, which was said to afflict and hold back England's neighbours in Europe.

Deeper exploration reveals the fallacies inherent in almost all of these arguments. Despite constant reiteration of the efficiency of capital-intensive English agriculture, rural England did not fare well during this century of supposed triumph. The country went from being a substantial food exporter in the first half of the 18th century to needing to import food from the 1790s on. Except for brief periods when war heightened demand, English agriculture suffered through extended depressions. Large-scale farmers did not do well, even with the price supports provided by the Corn Laws, which from 1815 to 1846–49 placed a sliding scale of tariffs on imported grain. After the end of the Corn Law price supports, English agriculture was severely strained and could not compete with imported grain from more efficient producers elsewhere. It remained depressed for most of the century.

More importantly, the century of the agricultural revolution deeply impoverished the majority of the English population: rural workers, cottagers and commoners. Proponents of agricultural improvement argued that it would lead to increased demand for agricultural labour and higher wages. As the *Economist* newspaper said in 1849, "high farming affords to the working man good wages and constant work."[8] The reality was very different. In the 1820s, William Cobbett, one of the most thoughtful commentators about rural life in the south of England, argued that farmers had devised a "scheme for squeezing rents out of the bones of the labourer," and as a consequence had reduced labourers' wages "so low, as to make the labourer a walking skeleton."[9] Or as Mary Ferris reported at a meeting of labourers protesting low wages in Bremhill, Wiltshire, in 1844: "Her children were often crying around her for food, and she did not know how to get any …. the men brought the 8 (shillings) home on a Saturday night, but the management was left to the women, who could not supply the wants for the families from it."[10]

Despite the *Economist*'s wishful words, agricultural wages (high farming or not), especially in the south of England, declined precipitously over the whole century. By the middle of the 19th century, real agricultural wages in the south of England were at least one third lower than they had been in the middle of the 18th century. Work was harder to find and of shorter duration — particularly for women — compared to a century earlier.[11]

Even more important in the declining fortunes of the rural poor was their increased dependence on wages as common lands were enclosed and cottagers denied access to the small pieces of land they, like Brinton Abbot, often turned into marvels of productivity and some measure of independence for the family. Over this century, Parliament passed 5,000 private enclosure bills affecting over seven million acres of common land. In some instances, enclosure simply replaced open-field land strips with more consolidated farms, even for smallholders. More often, however, enclosure reduced the circumstances and livelihoods of those holding only moderate common rights by restricting access to pasture and forest land. Enclosure simply impoverished those who had no common right but had relied on informal access to common "wastes" and woods for fuel and forage, and for customs such as that permitting gleaning of missed grain in harvested fields.

More devastating for the rural poor was the attack on cottages and cottage garden land. Throughout the century, a long list of knowledgeable commentators decried this "war on cottages" and the resultant distress. The Reverend David Davies, writing about his parish in Barkham, Berkshire, in 1782, argued that rich farmers were turning cottages into crowded tenements with no access to garden land. With reduced wages, his parishioners were nonetheless required to purchase more to meet their needs. The result was a downward spiral of poverty. As Davies said, "The depriving the peasantry of all landed property has beggared multitudes. ... Thus an amazing number of people have been reduced from a comfortable state of partial independence to the precarious condition of hirelings."[12] There was similar commentary in the decades to follow. Through the century of the oft-heralded agricultural revolution in England, "of improved agriculture of such industry that it is wonderful to relate," according to Fussell, the majority of people in England were driven to desperate levels of deprivation. Workers were forced to rely ever more heavily on wages for their survival. Real wages, not coincidentally, were constantly being reduced and employment was more sporadic and temporary. What had once been yearly employment became seasonal, daily or even hourly, and workers became fully dependent on the whims of the farmer and the market.

Even the Poor Law Commission of 1832–1834, notoriously unsympathetic to the rural poor, argued, "We can do little or nothing to prevent pauperism; the farmers will have it." Keeping the rural poor dependent on wages "enables them [farmers] to dismiss and resume their labourers according to their daily or even hourly want of them, to reduce the wages to the minimum, or even below the minimum of what will support an unmarried man."[13] In the 1830s, the *Times* newspaper, reporting on the arsons that formed the most obvious aspect of the Captain Swing uprisings, said: "The labourer has been literally ground down to the very dust."[14] Fourteen years later, in a series of articles commenting on yet another string of fires, the paper laid the blame for the unrest on low wages and the refusal to provide cottage land: "The farmer," it said, "looks at them [the labourer] as he does his horses — as animals out of whom he must get so much work at as little cost as possible."[15] Or as the *Times* remarked, "Of a truth there is something rotten in our state of England."[16]

"A Robust and Flourishing Peasantry"

It needn't have been so. There is little doubt that population growth stressed food production in England. The resultant increase in the price of grain contributed to falling real wages. War with France for close to two decades near the end of the 18th century and into the 19th, along with a series of bad harvests at the end of the 18th century, heightened the distress. Through the worst of these years, widespread hunger and malnutrition stalked the land. England, however, suffered through more than seven decades of poverty and hunger that cannot easily be blamed on the specifics of harvests and war. As late as 1864, one report to Parliament claimed that half of the agricultural labourers were chronically malnourished because of an absolute lack of food.[17] So much for the miraculous productivity stemming from the agricultural revolution.

Rural poverty deepened and food supplies became stressed despite a chorus arguing that providing cottagers with land would result in more food, less poverty and less rural unrest. Important among them were Arthur Young, William Cobbett and William Thomas Thornton.

Young was the best known and the most conflicted. He was born in 1741, the son of a minor member of the rural gentry. His father was the rector of Bradfield church in Suffolk and the family had for over 200 years owned a reasonably sized estate there. Though Young failed in his own attempts at farming — as he said, he "squandered much money, under golden dreams of improvements"[18] — a long career of writing about agriculture meant that he was, as one biographer said, "the most famous authority on agriculture in the English-speaking world."[19] Starting with his 1767 *Farmer's Letters to the People of England,* Young wrote an immense number of books and pamphlets on agricultural change. In 1784 he began his most ambitious publication, *The Annals of Agriculture, and Other Useful Arts,* which ran until 1806. Young wrote about a third of the content in the forty-six volumes of *Annals;* the rest consisted of reports and letters on agricultural subjects sent to him, usually from substantial landowners. In 1793, he was named Secretary to the Board of Agriculture and Internal Improvement, a semi-public board of members of the nobility and large landowners dedicated to fostering agricultural improvement and enclosure. Young served in this role until his death in 1820.

For most of this time, he was a faithful servant to large landowners and a dedicated proponent of agricultural improvement and enclosure. He dismissed arguments about increased poverty, blamed the poor for their poverty when he noticed it and warned landlords to be vigilant against rural unrest. A travel book published shortly before the outbreak of the

French Revolution turned Young quite unexpectedly into an authority on France. He used his authority to vigorously urge landowners in England to form a landed cavalry to guard against unrest designed to prompt "the democratic mischief of transferring property."[20] Young's yeoman cavalry was used in a notoriously brutal fashion to put down rural unrest for the next three decades.

Young was most exercised about the need for agricultural improvement, by which he meant enclosing common lands, investing capital in improving the land, charging high rents to large-scale tenants — who were also to invest substantial capital — and experimenting with new crops and fertilizers. He was also often opposed to providing people with access to small amounts of land. As he said in his *Travels in France*, small peasant holdings led to a "multiplication of wretchedness." He was, as one biographer praised, "the untiring and eloquent apostle for the Agricultural Revolution."[21]

But a funny thing happened on the way to the revolution. By the mid-1790s, Young, who perhaps travelled the countryside more than any other person writing in England at the time, was becoming increasingly concerned about deepening poverty. He was not alone in this; a number of large landowners who were also members of the Board of Agriculture became alarmed and linked such poverty to increased dependence on inadequate wages. Young encouraged members of the board to provide him with their opinions about the benefits of providing small amounts of land to the rural poor.[22] The result was a flood of detailed reports about the benefits of such land and eloquent testimony to the productivity and industriousness of such small peasant proprietors.

One of the earliest such reports was sent to the board by the Earl of Winchilsea in 1795. Winchilsea was a prominent member of the board with a 13,000-acre estate in Westwell, Kent. He said that on his estate labourers were guaranteed the secure rent of small plots of land for a garden and for keeping cows. By his account, even a rood of land would allow the family to grow most of what they consumed, make them "more fit to endure labour" and provide them "a sort of independence, which makes them set a higher value on their character." Moreover, according to Winchilsea, they would pay as much for the land as large tenant farmers. His comments were, no doubt, paternalistic and as concerned with reducing the costs of poor relief as they were with the welfare of the labourers. Nonetheless, his account helped provoke a fuller discussion of the productivity of peasant agriculture. Young published Winchelsea's observations in *Annals*, adding the following note: "As land cultivated as a garden will produce a greater quantity of food for man than in any other way, … it may not be too much to say, that 100,000 acres allotted cottagers as garden ground, will give a produce equal to what 150,000 acres cultivated in the ordinary way would give."[23]

Sir Henry Vavasour suggested the difference between peasant gardens and "ordinary" farming was much greater than Young had suggested. Vavasour provided the example of one man, Thomas Rook, who rented three acres on Vavasour's estate in Yorkshire. The land was farmed by Rook, his wife (unnamed in the account) and their twelve-year-old daughter. They kept two cows and two pigs and made the entire cost of rent in butter. Vavasour concluded,

> It is very evident that this man clears from his three acres more than a farmer can possibly lay by from more than eighty acres of land in the common husbandry of the country … and it must be obvious to everyone how great the advantages must be to society by cultivating land in this manner.[24]

A long string of such accounts was sent to the board and published by Young. Almost without exception, they stressed the dual benefits that flowed from such small peasant holdings: abundant production from very small plots of land and the substantial gains that families derived from the partial independence and modest well-being such land provided. One particularly detailed account was provided by Sir William Pulteney, one of the wealthiest members of the Board of Agriculture. He described a very small piece of garden land on his estate that a couple had maintained in secure rent for the last thirty-eight years. They were unnamed, but the man was a collier and the woman did most of the work on the land. They paid three shillings in rent and had raised six children on the land. The woman planted corn, potatoes and a large array of garden crops. She also raised a pig, purchased young in February, fattened from kitchen scraps and garden waste and sold in January. She kept no land in fallow and got better yields than the larger farmers around her. With sustained care over the years, what had started out as very poor land was improved. Pulteney attributed the woman's success to her intimate knowledge of her plot and to hard work: she instantly dispatched weeds; she developed a routine for seeding wheat along with digging up potatoes; and she fertilized the garden whenever she could with compost and manure, even collecting manure from the road.[25]

Pulteney's account was echoed by T. Babington. He argued that the small plots of land he rented out, mostly to labourers on his estate, "improved faster than that occupied by the generality of my more wealthy tenants. The former have always plans afoot for increasing the fertility of their little spots." Babington concluded that through such land, "an important addition is made to that useful class of men, the labour of whose hands fully supplies them with necessaries and decent comforts, and whose well employed capital and good habits render them a robust and flourishing peasantry."[26]

In 1800, Young added his voice to these discussions. His *An Inquiry into the Propriety of Applying Wastes to the Better Maintenance and Support of the Poor* was partly a condemnation of the way enclosure had deprived the poor of land. Although he supported the enclosure of common lands until his death, he was increasingly convinced that it had functioned to deprive the poor of land. He argued that this was neither necessary for the process of enclosure nor beneficial to society. Poverty was increasing dramatically, as was the cost of poor relief. The remedy for this, Young asserted, was to ensure with each enclosure act that enough land was set aside for a garden patch, potato land and sufficient hay land to keep a cow, and that all were inalienably attached to each cottage. This would not only relieve poverty but lead to a dramatic increase in production due to the prodigious industry of such smallholders: "To become independent, to marry a girl and fix her in a spot they can call their own, instigates a conduct, not a trace of which would be seen with the motive never in view. With this powerful impulse they ... will call into life and vigour every principle of industry."[27]

What are we to make of these accounts? They can be seen as self-serving, driven as they were by diverse impulses, not least the desire to reduce the cost of poor relief paid by large landowners and farmers. Self-provisioning could also be seen as a means for reducing wages below the necessary replacement cost for the worker and family. But it would be unwise to dismiss these accounts on that basis.

We have other accounts of peasant productivity to support their descriptions. Historians Joan Thirsk and Malcolm Thick have provided us with detailed histories of the efficiency of farming those small plots of land in various regions of England, in some instances centuries before the agricultural revolution. Joan Thirsk's descriptions of small garden plots in the South Midlands demonstrated that seven acres of land employed in labour-intensive agriculture could both provide for a family and produce a multitude of crops for the market. Thirsk argued that it was commonplace for those writing on agriculture in the early 1700s to assert that such gardeners "produced ten times more food than farmers from the same ground." She also suggested that it was the innovations of such small producers that would later be incorporated into aspects of "high" agriculture. Commentators in the early 1700s asserted that small farms planted with turnips, carrots, cabbages and other vegetable crops produced as much food as fifty acres of the general husbandry. Malcolm Thick reported that one acre of market garden near London employed ten people full time, and an additional twenty-five workers at peak harvest. These gardens were bursting with harvests of parsnips, carrots, turnips, cabbages, peas, beans, cucumbers, radishes, lettuces, asparagus, celery and with small fruit bushes and trees. The genesis of Wrigley's "advanced organic agriculture" lies most obviously in such small-scale production, not in high agriculture.[28]

This accords with many other descriptions of the complexity of peasant agriculture in England in this period. In 1801, Arthur Young published a "Cottager's Garden Calendar" in *Annals*. His discussion of what went into a successful cottager's garden, drawn from his observations in various parts of England, was noteworthy for the complexity of such gardens and the range of crops. Young suggested dates for planting radishes, parsley, beans, cabbages, shallots, chives, leeks, carrots, potatoes, turnips, onions, parsnips and kidney beans. He advised keeping bees — "three hives being often worth as much as your rent" — and pigs, and manuring and fertilizing with almost everything that came from the kitchen.[29] Young's description of the remarkable diversity in peasant holdings did not stand alone; a series of commentators provided similarly long lists of the products in a successful peasant garden. Charles Hall, after a life as a physician to the poor in the county of Devon, provided a ringing endorsement of small farming productivity. Arguing that "the produce of the land is proportionate to the labour bestowed on it," he suggested that three to three and a half acres would suffice to provide sustenance to a family of five. His list of the products from a cottage garden was almost as full as Young's and included wheat, barley, potatoes, turnips, peas, calico corn, flax, cabbage and beets.[30] Even commentators opposed to peasant agriculture admitted that such farming would relieve poverty. One of the estate owners to whom Young addressed his question reported that a family could live comfortably from a few acres of garden land, selling vegetables in local markets. John Boys saw this as an argument for not allowing them such land. He said, "When a labourer in this part of Kent is put into the possession of three or four acres of land, his labour is, in a great measure, lost to the community."[31] One wonders exactly what Boys meant by "the community" in this statement.

William Cobbett, a distinctive voice in early 19th-century England, also provided often detailed and glowing descriptions of peasant livelihoods. A farm boy from Farnham, Surrey, he spent some time in what is now Canada after joining the army somewhat accidentally. Upon leaving the army, he began a campaign against institutional corruption and the mistreatment of soldiers. These experiences drew him inexorably to life as a journalist and radical politician. Despite regular publishing exploits and time spent in exile in America, in jail and in Parliament, his dream for most of his life was to find a farm and a home reminiscent of his family's in Farnham. He eventually bought such a farm in Botley, "the most delightful village in the world. ... it has neither workhouse nor barber nor attorney nor justice of the peace."[32]

Cobbett spent a great deal of time commenting on life in the countryside, mostly discussing growing poverty. In the early 1800s, while searching for a farm to purchase, he came across the 150 acres of common land in Horton Heath. This small piece of common land was used to pasture the animals of wealthier farmers who had purchased stints, or the right to graze cattle, there. On the periphery of the commons, however, there were thirty cottages. With no common right, the cottagers had nonetheless scratched together little bits of land on which, according to Cobbett's count, they raised more than a hundred beehives, sixty pigs, fifteen cows and 500 poultry and grew a multitude of crops on their garden plots. As Cobbett said, "My calculation was that the cottages produced from their little bits in food, for themselves, and in things to be sold at market, *more than any neighbouring farm of 200 acres!*" At a later date, when Cobbett attempted to get the neighbouring estate owner, the Bishop of Winchester, to set aside some tiny plots of land for poor parishioners, he discovered:

> Not a single man [that is farmers in the parish] would agree to my proposal! One, bullfrog farmer [that is, a farmer who swallowed up smaller farms in a single gulp] ... said it would only make them *saucy!* And one, a true disciple of *Malthus*, said, that to facilitate their rearing of children *was a harm!* This man had ... land that had formerly been *six farms*.

Cobbett denounced a political and social system that could countenance such nonsense. As he said, "The cottages consisted, fathers, mothers, and children, and grandfathers, grandmothers and grandchildren, *of more than two hundred persons.* ... What a system must that have been that could lead *English* gentlemen to disregard matters like these!"[33]

Along with denouncing such disregard for the poor, Cobbett also became a vocal proponent of the cottage economy. His 1823 book *Cottage Economy* was a ringing endorsement of the peasant family's self-reliance, exemplified by their ability to supply themselves with the necessities of life. One of 19th-century England's crimes, Cobbett believed, was that having deprived cottagers of both land for their gardens and pigs and wood or peat as fuel from common "wastes," they could no longer produce these things for themselves. It was also almost surely Cobbett who penned a long, anonymous lament to the *Times* in 1830. In this, the writer observed that, "before the breaking up of the small farms," the labourer would have his cottage and his cottage garden and a life:

> At that period, the peasant, when the ... labours of the day were closed ... wended his way to his own snug little cottage, and partook of an ample though frugal meal in the company of his wife and children ... he would then hie to his patch of garden ground ... O, it was a beautiful picture of contented toil, steady loyalty, parental affection and faithful love ... Then a peasant had something to live for.... But, alas the scene is sadly changed now .... Then sounded the knell of the English peasant's comforts .... Then first began the grinding system which has since crushed the peasantry, to even the marrow and the bones ... his piggery, his little patch of garden ground, and his right of common, were wrenched from him by the strong grip of avarice in power, and were added to the acres of the gentleman farmer.[34]

"The Occult Principle of the System"

Despite the misgivings of Young and some of the landowners in the Board of Agriculture, and despite the eloquence of Cobbett, the obvious evidence of increased poverty and the almost continuous opposition of the rural poor, the prophets of the agricultural revolution continued to dominate both policy and polemic in England through the first half of the 19th century. They were encouraged in their attack on peasant agriculture by the constant references to the magic of capital from authors purporting to reveal the secrets of a new "science": political economy.

The first few decades of the 19th century witnessed a proliferation of publications attempting to explain the route to what Adam Smith had labelled "universal opulence." Using Smith's 1776 *An Inquiry into the Nature and Causes of the Wealth of Nations* as their touchstone, a long list of authors produced works meant to explain "the principles of political economy." The most important British authors among them included the Reverend Thomas Robert Malthus, his good friend David Ricardo, Nassau Senior, John McCulloch, James Mill and John Stuart Mill. While they often disagreed on important aspects of political economy, they tended to converge around a set of tropes that defined the science.

The most important of these was the purported magic of capital. All of them argued that it was labour chained to capital that unlocked the potential for economic growth and prosperity. As Smith said in *Wealth*, it was the attempt to employ capital in the most advantageous fashion that constituted the "invisible hand" that promoted public well-being.[35] Malthus was even more adamant about the importance of both political economy and capital. In 1803, he argued in typically stilted fashion, "Political economy is perhaps the only science, of which it may be said that the ignorance of it is not merely a deprivation of good, but produces great positive evil."[36] And in 1820, he asserted that the key to the increase of wealth was the accumulation of capital and its "power of commanding ... labour."[37] Not only was capital the source of wealth, but in the hands of political economists such wealth also became the basis of morality, indeed of all natural laws. Nassau Senior, perhaps most directly, argued that the "pursuit of wealth ... is the great source of moral improvement" and cautioned that any impediment to the accumulation of wealth would lead not just to increased poverty but to social disintegration.[38]

Not everyone was so enamoured of the arguments in favour of capital. A string of critics warned that the reification of capital was leading both to impoverishment and to increased repression. As Charles Hall suggested:

> As the condition of the poor grows worse ... coercive measures will increase, the laws securing property will be multiplied and rendered more severe .... To keep people that are cold, naked and hungry from taking fuel to warm themselves, clothes to cover themselves with, and food to satisfy their hunger (means) ... inflicting punishments greater than the sufferings of the poor.[39]

Perhaps the most interesting of these critiques was a work written under a pseudonym, Piercy Ravenstone, in 1821. (The writer's true identity was never established.) Ravenstone described a system in which the "occult principle of the system" — capital — was used as a talisman to justify increased poverty. Capital, he argued,

> serves to account for whatever cannot be accounted for in any other way. Where reason fails, where argument is insufficient, it operates like a talisman to silence all doubts. ... it is the great mother of all things, it is the cause of every event that happens in the world. ... It is the deity of their idolatry which they have set up to worship in the high places of the Lord; and were its powers what they imagine, it would not be unworthy of their adoration ...

[Instead, Ravenstone warned,] "The tree of their wealth is planted in the bowels of the poor. The fruits it bears are watered with their blood and their tears."[40]

Despite such critics, in 1843 the *Economist* was established and soon began extolling the wonders of capital. The newspaper was also a powerful voice opposing land for the rural poor. The second edition, in September 1843, celebrated the fact that agricultural improvement was at work in the countryside, "breaking up the hard clods of ignorance, prejudice, sloth and indifference ... the *art* of husbandry, is rapidly changing into the *science* of agriculture."[41] But it was premature to celebrate the transition from art to science. For the next two decades, the *Economist* was preoccupied with the depressed condition of English agriculture and sought to inspire policies that would solve what it determined to be the pre-eminent problem in rural England: "How can capital be attracted to the soil?"[42]

In its efforts to champion a view of agriculture that would treat land "simply as an object of commercial enterprise,"[43] the paper vehemently opposed any movement to provide the rural poor with land — no matter how productive they could be. In reaction to a campaign to provide rural labourers with garden allotments — inspired to some extent by a renewed outbreak of rural arson in the 1840s — the *Economist* vigorously denounced such schemes, arguing that they would "stagnate labour exactly on those spots where it is least needed." As the paper said, "A pursuit ... for which the capitalist cannot pay wages should be instantly abandoned."[44] It combined this opposition with constant denunciations of peasant or small-scale agriculture.

The *Economist* was most incensed by the work of two authors in the second half of the 1840s. In 1845, William Thomas Thornton — soon to be a close associate of John Stuart Mill in the East India Company office — published a compelling attack on one of the principle arguments against peasant agriculture: the assertion, most often attributed to Robert Malthus, that it would lead to rapid population increase. In this work, *Over-Population and Its Remedy,* Thornton argued that Malthus had the cause and effect of population increase all wrong. It was misery, Thornton argued, that led to rapid population increase. In a survey of peasant livelihoods in various regions of Europe, Thornton asserted that an equitable division of land in modest holdings both led to rural comfort and insured against a rapid population increase, as those favoured by such comfort were not likely to squander it through "matrimonial imprudence."[45]

Thornton followed this up in 1848 with a more extensive work on peasant productivity entitled *A Plea for Peasant Proprietors*. In this, he examined both peasant well-being and productivity in those locations in Europe where very small peasant proprietors continued to have access to land: Flemish Belgium, Guernsey and the Channel Islands, Norway and Germany.

Thornton's careful depiction of peasant lives in these locales helped him make a strong case that land held in very small farms both produced the most food and led to more harmonious societies. Unlike the scenes of rural violence in Britain, he argued, in all of the locations where peasant proprietors predominated, there "are no rick-burners, no breakers of thrashing machines, no riots among the country people, and no secret disaffection."[46]

Thornton's work served as both a strong endorsement of peasant productivity and a ringing condemnation of the infatuation with capital and agricultural improvement then prevalent in England. It would not, however, have had the impact it did were it not for the fact that it strongly influenced the work of Thornton's officemate, John Stuart Mill. Though he continued to work as a reader for the East India Company's Board of Control, by the second half of the 1840s, John Stuart Mill was probably the most influential political economist in Britain. His 1848 publication, *Principles of Political Economy,* helped burnish that reputation. While much of Mill's *Principles* differed little from more established works on political economy, he vigorously supported Thornton's views on the benefits of peasant proprietors. Mill argued that British writers ignored assertions about the benefits of very small-scale farming because they were unfamiliar with peasant life and "have almost always the most erroneous ideas of their social condition and mode of life."[47] Mill cited Thornton extensively in his work, along with many other travellers and agricultural writers, including Arthur Young. Young had meant his work on French agriculture to testify to the benefits of agricultural improvement and large farms. But even in this early work — before his embrace of the poor — he occasionally let his powers of observation overcome his prejudices. In his *Travels in France,* he had commented favourably about peasant properties around Béarn, noting that these farms and small orchards were "nursed up with so much care that nothing but the fostering attention of the owner could effect anything like it." Elsewhere in the book, he had commented on how peasants "turn their rocks into scenes of fertility, because I suppose THEIR OWN," and later, "The magic of property turns sand to gold."[48]

Mill also rejected arguments that peasant holdings led to rapid population increase, suggesting that despite prejudices to the contrary, he was not able to find any single "authentic instance" to support that argument. Finally, Mill concluded:

No other existing state of agricultural economy has so beneficial an effect on the industry, the intelligence, the frugality, and prudence of the population ... and that no existing state, therefore, is on the whole so favourable both to their moral and physical welfare.[49]

In response to his assertion about the benefits of peasant agriculture, the *Economist* published a series of increasingly virulent articles opposing both Mill and such small-scale agriculture. The paper argued that all the examples Mill provided "prove the painful frugality and unremitting and ill-rewarded toil" of peasants, and it summarized its understanding of progress as

the division of the classes dependent upon the land, into proprietors, tenants, and farm-labourers, ... will be found to be an important step in the progress of civilisation ... constant and regularly paid agricultural wages will conduce more to the comfort and advancement of our labourers than the precarious independence of peasant farming.[50]

Peasant agriculture was, according to the paper, "a wasteful and retrograde misapplication of human labour," especially when compared to the wonderful productivity of labour "when employed in connection with capital and in combination with other labourers under the superintendence of a capitalist with skill and enterprise."[51] After the release of the 1851 census indicating for the first time that a majority of people in England lived in towns, the *Economist* crowed that such changes had "broken down the parochial and patriarchal barriers which made each spot of land a gaol, though a home, for a particular portion of the community, and the same progress will cause them to be entirely removed."[52]

"A Sweet Habit of the Blood"

This was a strange definition of progress, perhaps, given the continued poverty in rural England. Two detailed reports in the 1860s outlined clearly the extent of that poverty. In 1864, the first national survey of cottagers' living conditions reported that each inhabitant had less than one third of the space mandated as a bare minimum per person in the much-despised workhouses. That same year, a report by Dr. E. Smith to Parliament asserted that close to half the population in agricultural districts was chronically malnourished because of an absolute lack of food.[53]

Through more than a century of dispossession and repression, peasants and rural labourers in England and Wales tenaciously stuck to the land, proving that their little bits were always more a "home" than a "gaol." At the beginning of the 19th century, Arthur Young argued, "Nothing can be clearer than the vast importance which all these poor people, scattered as they are through so many counties, and affected by circumstances so extremely various, attach to the object of possessing land, though no more than to set a cottage on."[54] A couple of decades later, William Cobbett argued that a good life was most obviously constructed from the modest needs of a peasant household, providing themselves with as much of their necessities as they could, especially his trinity of bread, beer and bacon. As Cobbett asserted, "A couple of flitches of bacon are worth fifty thousand Methodist sermons," counselling hard work and diligence in paid labour.[55] A half-century later, between a half and a quarter of rural households still kept a pig. As Walter Rose remarked in his recollections of English village life from the 1870s and 1880s, "Life without a pig was almost unthinkable."[56] Seven decades after Young argued for the importance of the parish and little bits of land, George Eliot in *Daniel Deronda* could still comment, "A human life, I think, should be well rooted in some spot of a native land, where it may get the love of tender kinship for the peace of earth, for the labors men go forth to." The spot, she suggests, is one where working the land together spreads "kindly acquaintance with all neighbors ... as a sweet habit of the blood."[57]

The craft of getting the most from small bits of land was most often hard-won and built from peasants' experience. No doubt their lives seemed harsh to writers with little understanding of peasants; their labour "clumsy," as the *Economist* said. But, as George Sturt wrote about the cottagers around Farnham at the beginning of the 20th century, it was through this "home-made civilization of the rural English" that people could find "not only a method of getting a living, but also an encouragement and a help to live well."[58] Had the unrelenting self-reliance Sturt described been encouraged instead of attacked in the name of progress and capital, one hundred years of desperate poverty would surely have been relieved.

NOTES

1   *Economist*, "Rebecca Riots," 1:7 (Oct. 14, 1843) 105.

2   Reprinted in the *Times*, June 14, 1844, 6.

3   In England in the 18th and 19th century, "peasant" was a label most often applied to farm labourers with access to cottage land (usually rented), although the mix of wage labour and their own agricultural pursuits varied markedly. The smallest yeoman farmers were also labelled "peasants."

4   G.E. Fussell, "My Impressions of Arthur Young," *Agricultural History Review* 17 (1943), 135–144, esp. 144.

5   "Re-establishing the English Agricultural Revolution," *Agricultural History Review*

44 (1996), 1–20, esp. 20; see also Overton's *Agricultural Revolution in England: The Transformation of the Agrarian Economy, 1500–1850,* Cambridge: Cambridge University Press, 1996, esp. 116–117; E.A. Wrigley, *Energy and the English Industrial Revolution,* Cambridge: Cambridge University Press, 2010, esp. 29; M.E. Turner, J.V. Beckett and B. Afton, *Farm Production in England, 1700–1914,* Oxford: Oxford University Press, 2001, esp. 230; Peter Jones, *Agricultural Enlightenment: Knowledge, Technology, and Nature,* Oxford: Oxford University Press, 2016.

6   For a fuller discussion, see Jim Handy, "'Almost Idiotic Wretchedness': A Long History of Blaming Peasants," *Journal of Peasant Studies* 36:2 (2009), 325–344.

7   E.A. Wrigley, *Continuity, Chance, Change: The Character of the Industrial Revolution in England,* Cambridge: Cambridge University Press, 2004; Robert Allen, "The Nitrogen Hypothesis and the English Agricultural Revolution: A Biological Analysis," *Journal of Economic History* 68 (2008), 182–210; Colin Duncan, *The Centrality of Agriculture,* Montreal: McGill-Queens Press, 1996.

8   *Economist,* "Employment of Labour in Husbandry," 7:229 (May 19, 1849), 547.

9   William Cobbett, *Rural Rides in the Counties of Surrey, Kent, Hampshire, etc.* London: np, 1830, 30, 28.

10   Cited in the *Economist,* "Provinces," 2:57 (Sept. 28, 1844), 1259.

11   There is a complex and sophisticated literature exploring English agricultural wages during this century. Marx argued real rural wages fell 25 percent between 1737 and 1777, and a further 45 percent between 1771 and 1808. Marx, *Capital Vol. 1,* 675. These early arguments by Marx have been mostly borne out in further research. In 1955, H. Phelps Brown and S.V. Hopkins provided an estimate of real agricultural wages in England and Wales asserting that from a level of 100 in 1730, wages declined to 72 by 1800. Keith Snell has taken these arguments further and estimated that in southern England real wages fell by 20 percent between 1750 and 1833, and fell to 79 percent of their 1833 average by 1851. See H. Phelps Brown and S.V. Hopkins, "Seven Centuries of Building Wages," *Economica* 24 (1955), 296–314; Keith Snell, *Annals of the Labouring Poor: Social Change and Agrarian England, 1600–1900,* Cambridge: Cambridge University Press, 1985, 37.

12   David Davies, *The Case of Labourers in Husbandry Stated and Considered,* London: G.G. and J. Richardson, 1795, esp. 52, 33–34, 73–74, 135–136.

13   Cited in S.G. and E.O.A. Checkland (eds.), *The Poor Law Report of 1834,* Harmondshire: Penguin, 1974, 279–280, 135.

14   *Times,* Oct. 30, 1830, 3.

15   *Times,* March 23, 1844, 5; June 7, 1844, 6; June 10, 1844, 7; June 11, 1844, 5; June 14, 1844, 6.

16   *Times,* March 23, 1844, 6.

17   *Economist,* "The Food of the English Labourer," 22:102 (Oct. 8, 1864), 1252–1253.

18   Arthur Young, "Memoirs of the Last Thirty Years of the Editor's Farming Life," *Annals of Agriculture, and Other Useful Arts* 15 (1791), 152–182, esp. 154.

19   John G. Gazley, *The Life of Arthur Young,* Philadelphia: American Philosophical Society, 1973, 306.

20 Arthur Young, *Travels in France during the Years 1787, 1788, and 1789*, ed. Constancia Maxwell, Cambridge: Cambridge University Press, 1950, 347.

21 Gazley, *The Life of Arthur Young*, 1973, 1.

22 Young was deeply affected by the death of his youngest daughter in 1797 and subsequently embraced religious dissent. This heightened his concern for the poor, but he had begun publishing articles about the need to provide the poor with land two years before his daughter's death.

23 Earl of Winchilsea, "On the Advantages of Cottagers Renting Land," *Annals* 26 (1796), 227–245.

24 Included in Sir John Sinclair, "Observations on the Means of Enabling a Cottager to Keep a Cow by the Produce of a Small Portion of Arable Land," *Annals* 36 (1800), 231–248.

25 Sir William Pulteney, "Accounts of Cottagers," *Annals of Agriculture* 44 (1806), 97–111.

26 Ibid.

27 Arthur Young, *An Inquiry into the Propriety of Applying Wastes for the Better Maintenance and Support of the Poor*, London, np. 1801, esp. 7, 12, 42–43; this was also printed in *Annals* 36 (1800), 497–547.

28 Joan Thirsk, "Agricultural Innovations and their Diffusion," 533–589 in Thirsk (ed.), *The Agrarian History of England and Wales, Vol. 5: 1640–1740*, Cambridge: Cambridge University Press, 1985, 585; Joan Thirsk, "Agricultural Policy: Public Debate and Legislation," 298–388 in ibid.; Malcolm Thick, "Market Gardening In England and Wales," 503–532 in ibid., 511, 515; Joan Thirsk, "The Southwest Midlands," 159–196 in Thirsk (ed.), *The Agrarian History of England and Wales, Vol. I, Regional Farming Systems*, Cambridge, Cambridge University Press, 1984, 170–171.

29 Arthur Young, "Cottager's Garden Calendar," *Annals of Agriculture* 36 (1801), 145–147.

30 Charles Hall, *The Effects of Civilisation on the People of the European States*, London: John Minter Morgan, 1849 (reprint of the 1805 edition), 230–239.

31 John Boys, "Crops and Poor," *Annals of Agriculture* 36 (1800), 368–370.

32 William Cobbett, *The Autobiography of William Cobbett*, London: Faber and Faber Ltd., 1962, 9, 99.

33 William Cobbett, *Cottage Economy*, London, 1823, 144; see also William Cobbett, *The Autobiography of William Cobbett* (ed. William Reitzell), London: Faber and Faber Ltd., 1962, 107–108.

34 "The Peasant's Friend," *Times*, Nov. 6, 1830, 3.

35 Adam Smith, *An Inquiry into the Nature and Causes of the Wealth of Nations*, Book IV, ch. Ii. London: W. Strahan, 1776. (Most often works on Smith reference this attempt to prove that Smith was talking about individual exertion, or supply and demand. It is very clear, though, that Smith was referring only to the use of capital in his lone mention of the "invisible hand" in *Wealth of Nations*.)

36 T.R. Malthus, *An Essay on the Principle of Population*, 1803 edition, vol. II, 152, fn. 10.

37 T.R. Malthus, *Principles of Political Economy*, 1989 [1820], 120.

38 See Nassau Senior, *An Introductory Lecture on Political Economy*, London: J.

Murray, 1831, 2, 7–8, 10; Nassau Senior, *Four Introductory Lectures on Political Economy,* London: J. Murray, 1847, 10, 11–12.

39 Charles Hall, *Effects,* 1849 [1805], 80, 181–182 (note at bottom).

40 Ravenstone, *A Few Doubts as to the Correctness of Some Opinions Generally Entertained on the Subjects of Population,* New York: Augustus M. Kelly, 1966, reprint of the 1821 edition, 292–294; 287–289. For further discussion about Ravenstone's identity, see Jim Handy, *Apostles of Inequality: Rural Poverty, Political Economy, and the Economist, 1760–1860,* Toronto: University of Toronto Press, 2022.

41 *Economist,* "Scientific Agriculture for Farmers," 1:2 (Sept. 9, 1843), 27.

42 *Economist,* "Agriculture: Land; Its Uses and Abuses," 4:150 (July 11, 1846), 893–894.

43 *Economist,* "Land: A Commodity," 7:303 (June 16, 1849), 659.

44 *Economist,* "The Labourer's Panacea — The Allotment System," 2:62 (Nov. 2, 1844), 1369–1370.

45 William Thornton, *Over-population and Its Remedy,* London: Longman, Brown, Green and Longmans, 1846, 121, 140–144, 207–208, 211. Note: Thornton coined this term in his 1848 book, but he used a similar argument throughout the 1845 one.

46 William Thornton, *A Plea for Peasant Proprietors,* London: MacMillan and Co., 1874 (first published, 1848), 175.

47 John Stuart Mill, *Principles of Political Economy, with Some of Their Applications to Social Philosophy,* London: George Routledge and Sons Ltd., 1848, 178–179.

48 Young, *Travels in France,* 1950, 54, 50, 88.

49 Mill, *Principles,* 1848, 204, 206.

50 *Economist,* "The Productiveness of Large and Small Farms," 6:274 (Nov. 25, 1848), 1330–1331.

51 *Economist,* "French Husbandry," 9:420 (Sept. 13, 1851), 1012–1013.

52 *Economist,* "Scarcity of Labour," 13:628 (Sept. 8, 1855), 979–980.

53 Alan Armstrong and J.P. Huzel, "Labour II: Food, Shelter, and Self-Help, the Poor Law and the Position of the Labourer in Rural Society," in G.E. Mingay (ed.) *The Agrarian History of England and Wales Vol. VI,* Cambridge: Cambridge University Press, 1985, 729–835; *Economist,* "The Food of the English Labourer," 22:1102 (Oct. 8, 1864), 1252–1253.

54 Arthur Young, *An Inquiry into the Propriety of Applying Wastes,* 1801, 11.

55 William Cobbett, *Cottage Economy,* London, 1823, 139.

56 Walter Rose, *Good Neighbours: Some Recollections of an English Village and Its People,* Cambridge: Cambridge University Press, 1964, 65.

57 Cited in Keith Snell, *Parish and Belonging: Community, Identity and Welfare in England and Wales, 1700–1950,* Cambridge: Cambridge University Press, 2006, Preface.

58 George Sturt, *Change in the Village,* New York: George H. Doran Company, 1912, 117–125. (Written under his pseudonym, George Bourne.)

JAMAICA

Sugar Production

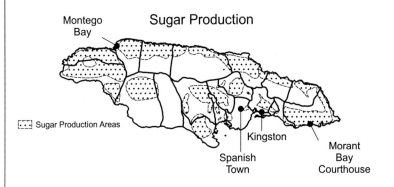

Montego
Bay

Sugar Production Areas

Kingston

Spanish
Town

Morant
Bay
Courthouse

Elevation

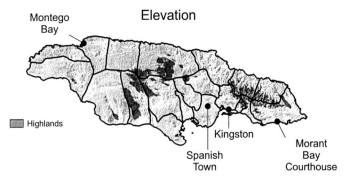

Montego
Bay

Highlands

Kingston

Spanish
Town

Morant
Bay
Courthouse

● Important Locations

☐ 1804 Parish Boundaries

0   25   50 km

3 Jamaican Peasants in Slavery, Semi-Slavery and Freedom

In 1842, Neill Malcolm provided testimony to the House of Commons Select Committee on the West India Colonies. The committee had been established in 1834 to investigate relations between Black labourers and sugar estates in Jamaica, less than a decade after emancipation. Although Malcolm possessed "considerable property" in Jamaica, he had never been there; in anticipation of his appearance before the Select Committee, he had written to the agent who supervised his properties in Jamaica, Donald Sinclair. Malcolm read Sinclair's response to the committee. It said in part:

> The labourers in this island enjoy privileges, comforts and luxuries that I am sure no peasantry in Europe can command …. They raise hogs and poultry, and many of them horses; their gardens and grounds are very productive …. Besides this, almost every house has two or three bread-fruit trees with cocoa nut, orange and other fruit trees attached to it; the bread fruit alone is sufficient to support a family for two or three months of the year …. The market is entirely supplied by them with hogs and poultry …. They also supply the market with ground provisions, vegetables, and fruits …. They are fast gaining wealth and property; a great many have already purchased freeholds of their own.

This would appear to be a pleasing description of a prosperous peasant population, but this was neither Malcolm's nor Sinclair's intent. Instead, Sinclair cautioned that the prosperity of former slaves-turned-peasants made them "totally independent of their employer or of performing continuous field labour," and warned, "Many have also rented land, and have built huts upon it, and are squatting down, doing little or no labour for any estate."[1]

If England presented a picture of deepening rural poverty through a century of agricultural revolution — a century during which the rural poor were denied access to land for their own use to ensure large farmers had dependent and industrious labourers — Jamaica by the 1840s was often put forward as exemplifying the calamitous results of a prosperous peasantry. The many troubles of Jamaica's sugar industry were laid entirely at the feet of a reluctant or overly expensive workforce, newly freed from the chains of slavery. Jamaican peasants were tarred with the same brush as 19th century-labourers, their sins being indolence and independence.

By the 1850s, this purported reluctance to labour was increasingly described in racial terms: "negroes" would never be industrious on their own because they were incapable of developing increased wants-turned-into-needs that could inspire such energy and forethought. It became commonplace to argue that Jamaican peasants needed to be forced to labour, either through some form of direct compulsion or through laws and taxes that impoverished and forced them to feel the "beneficent whip of hunger and cold" as a substitute for the "spur of physical tyranny," as the *Economist* newspaper urged.[2] Increased attempts to make it harder for peasants to earn a living independent of wage labour led finally to a series of peasant protests that provoked a predictably violent response. Hundreds were killed in the aftermath of the Morant Bay "rebellion" and decades of anti-peasant legislation followed. Through this turmoil a few things remained constant: ex-slaves and their descendants turned gardens, small plots of land in former provision grounds and freehold estates, into remarkably productive enterprises, not only supplying themselves with necessities, but also feeding Jamaica itself through the island's vibrant markets.

Slave Gardens and Provision Grounds

Jamaica in the 18th century became the quintessential Caribbean colony: dominated by sugar, dependent on slavery, the bulk of the sugar estates owned by absentee landlords. The decade-long rebellion in neighbouring Saint-Domingue, which took place near the end of the century and eventually led to an independent Haiti, should have been a powerful warning to Jamaican sugar barons. Instead, no longer needing to compete with Saint-Domingue's sugar and coffee industries, Jamaican production increased dramatically. The number of slaves in Jamaica peaked at 354,000 in 1808, just as the prohibition against the transatlantic slave trade came into effect for British colonies.[3] Slavery dominated until emancipation in 1834.

Anyone familiar with the literature on plantation slavery will have no doubts about its brutality; Jamaica was, perhaps, particularly brutal. Richard Dunn argued that Jamaica demonstrated a "sugar and slave system in its starkest and most exploitive form."[4] The memoirs of Thomas Thistlewood, an estate manager and slave owner who arrived in Jamaica in 1750, are horrifying in their casual acknowledgement of constant violence. Thistlewood considered himself an enlightened man; he had one of the largest libraries on the island, read widely of the philosophers of the Enlightenment and was noted for his interest in agricultural improvement — yet he exhibited a shocking brutality towards his slaves. In his first year at an estate called Vineyard, Thistlewood whipped two thirds of the men and half of the women, and he invented even more horrific punishments, especially for runaway slaves. He forced himself on slave women at almost every opportunity.[5]

But even the most brutal regimes relied on certain levels of accommodation between masters and slaves. One such arrangement was described by Sinclair in the testimony that started this chapter. Slaves had access to garden plots — "home grounds" — surrounding their huts as well as to other provision grounds, which they used to grow both food for themselves, and increasingly, products for marketing. In Jamaica, where less than one sixth of the land held by sugar estates was in sugar, it made good sense for plantation owners seeking to reduce the cost of production to allow slaves to use both home gardens and provision grounds to grow food for themselves. But access to such land was soon considered a right, confirmed by custom and cherished by slaves. By the middle of the 18th century, chroniclers noted the sense of rightful ownership to hut, garden and provision grounds among slaves in Jamaica.[6] Following emancipation, attempts to interfere with such rights became an important element in heightening tensions between newly freed slaves and plantation owners.

The available evidence makes clear that both house gardens and provision grounds were highly productive. Each sizeable plantation would have a slave "village" of huts, most often built by the slaves themselves from readily available material or lumber, surrounded by small gardens of the most-used vegetables and fruit trees. These garden grounds, like the rood of land nurtured by Brinton Abbot described in the introduction, produced a remarkable range of foodstuffs. And like Abbot's multiple fruit trees, much of this came from permaculture. Alexander Barclay in 1827 described the gardens of slaves as "filled with plantains, ochras, and other vegetables … abound[ing] also with cocoa-nut and calabash trees."[7]

Although they often worked eighteen-hour days during the sugar harvest, slaves, like English cottagers tending their small plots after work, apparently tended to their home grounds whenever they could. When asked how much time slaves spent on their provision grounds and home gardens, William Taylor, in his testimony to the House of Commons Select Committee in preparation for emancipation, reported that they often spent their "shell blows" — their meal time intervals — working on their gardens.[8]

Slave gardens were important in feeding slave families and reducing the costs of provisioning for slaves. Yet it was in the provision grounds that slave agriculture became important to the overall economy of Jamaica. Provision grounds were most often a fair distance from the slave village, on mountainous or hilly land owned by the estate. Thus, unlike the garden, which could benefit from continuous attention, provision ground production was curtailed by the limited time slaves could devote to working the land. Distant provision grounds could not be visited at mealtimes, nor following many hours of work, nor could they be easily tended by children too young to work on the estate. Although some estate owners provided more, it was the custom by the end of the 18th century to allow slaves every second Saturday off to work on provision grounds.[9]

The limited labour that slaves could expend on their provision grounds was reflected in the size of their lots. Few planted more than an acre or two. Even with such limitations, however, commentators often expressed amazement at the amounts produced. William Beckford, writing in the 1780s about a provision plot, remarked that it was, "astonishing what quantities of the common necessaries of life it will produce. A quarter of an acre of this description will be fully sufficient for the supply of a moderate family, and may enable the proprietor to carry some to market besides."[10] What they grew on these lands was impressive. John Bigelow, though writing after a journey to Jamaica in the 1850s, argued that even during slavery, provision grounds provided apples, oranges, pomegranates, figs, cashews, bananas, dates, plantains, akee, breadfruit, mangoes, potatoes, yams, cassava roots, peas, and beans, ochro, choco, calalue, maize and calico corn.[11] Such remarkable productivity was due in equal parts to the fertility inherent in land newly reclaimed from forest and to the dynamic, eclectic mix of crops from America, Europe and Africa, all using every niche of land.

Slave gardens and provision grounds were so productive that slaves regularly had excess crops to sell. Thus, slave husbandry fed not only slaves in Jamaica but everyone else. Report after report from the mid-1700s and on talked about the bounty available in Jamaican markets and the essential role of slave husbandry in supplying them.

James Hakewill, the well-known painter and architect, after a stay of two years in Jamaica (1820 to 1821), assured his readers:

Nearly the whole of the markets of Jamaica are supplied with every species of vegetable and fruit by the overplus of the negro's produce, by which traffic they acquire considerable riches … these grumble as much at the low price of yams and plantains as an English farmer at the fall of corn.[12]

Alexander Barclay in 1827 also remarked on how slave husbandry was able to "alone supply all the markets of the island with [pigs and poultry]." Later, Barclay echoed Hakewill's sentiments in attempting to refute an argument that slaves were denied provisions. Barclay argued this could not be true because slaves "are not only the growers of their own food, but the farmers who supply the masters of the country with provisions; that the city of Kingston, and every town and shipping place around the island, is supplied from the surplus of their cultivation."[13]

Edward Long argued that the consequence of this production meant "industrious and frugal" slaves were able to accumulate significant wealth, and in the 1770s, "have the greatest part of the small silver circulating among them."[14] We need to approach these arguments about slave wealth with some caution, yet the reports of prodigious production and the surplus income that slaves and others could win from working the small plots of land intensely are too numerous to dismiss. William Taylor in 1832 provided the example of one freed slave who rented two acres of land. According to Taylor, he paid sixty shillings for the land. In addition, because his wife was a slave, he needed to pay £18 "rent" a year to her owner. Despite these costs, the couple were able to support themselves and two children solely on the income from his land.[15] The speed with which many ex-slaves were able to buy themselves out of apprenticeship after 1834 also suggests many were able to turn a substantial income from provision and home ground production.

There is overwhelming evidence of the productivity of slave husbandry, both for self-consumption and for the market, despite the terrible inhibitions resulting from the fact of their slavery. It is also clear that such industry had not gone unnoticed. Though most writing on Jamaican agriculture focused on sugar, commentators who lifted their eyes to slave gardens and provision grounds encountered industrious labourers/peasants cultivating remarkably productive lands. Yet, following emancipation in 1834 slaves who were once lauded for their industrious labour in house gardens and provision grounds were increasingly described as shirkers when they insisted on such work; their indolence imagined as a prelude to disaster. To understand this shift, it is necessary to return to familiar arguments from a different setting: the desperate need for dependent labourers and the challenge that peasants presented to the domination of capital.

"Land of Half Freedom" or "Saved from a Life of Savage Sloth"

The Jamaican sugar industry reached its peak of production in the early 1800s, after which it stagnated. Most often, Jamaican planters claimed that the end of the slave trade in British possessions in 1807-08 forced them to keep a larger percentage of "unproductive" slaves on estates to allow for a natural increase in the slave population, thereby increasing their costs. Though production per slave increased, fewer slaves were used in growing and processing cane as the 19th century progressed.[16] The temper of the colony also changed. The population was always heavily skewed towards Black and slave populations but it became even more so. In the decade between 1824 and 1834, the percentage of the population that was white fell by a half.[17]

This exodus accentuated a continuing problem in Jamaica: the predominance of absentee ownership. The parade of estate owners who had rarely or never been to Jamaica who testified to the various Select Committees on the West Indies through the 1830s and 1840s indicated the extent of the problem. Their reliance on the testimony of their estate managers, as Malcolm had needed to rely on Sinclair, provided evidence of further problems. Owners depended on a complex network of lawyers, estate managers and agents to run their estates. Even if all of these individuals were honest and industrious, the division of responsibility and the need to pay salaries or shares to multiple levels of managers reduced profits from the estates; what had once been a stream of considerable income to landed interests in England slowed to a trickle.

By the 1820s, many sugar estates were deeply in debt to merchants or bankers in England. Mortgages and encumbrances on estates reduced profits even further and many estate owners scrambled continually to pay mortgages. Encumbrances meant they were often compelled to market their crops through specific merchants and accept reduced prices.[18] Adding to their difficulties, in 1823 the House of Commons declared that it was Britain's intention to end slavery in its possessions as soon as it could safely and responsibly do so. While supporters of West Indian interests repeatedly managed to delay that day, planters argued that the resultant uncertainty had depreciated the value of estates and slaves, and had made it impossible to sell estates, and consequently, to negotiate new mortgages with bankers at better terms.[19]

However, the underlying problem had little to do with these issues. By the early 19th century, with Cuba, Mauritius and Louisiana emerging as important sugar producers, and with sugar production in Brazil revived, surplus sugar on the world markets was driving down prices. By the 1830s, planters were arguing that they could seldom make a profit from sugar production at current prices. All of these problems were apparent before the Great Jamaican Rebellion of 1831 galvanized public opinion toward the abolition of slavery in 1833 — to take effect on August 1, 1834.

This was a strange kind of freedom. The 1823 resolution had assured slave owners that an end to slavery would be accompanied by "a fair and equitable consideration of the interests of private property." Emancipation was also deeply entwined with concerns about the need to discipline a newly freed labour force to the demands of wage labour. The questions pursued by the Select Committee on the Extinction of Slavery through 1831 and 1832 demonstrated clearly these concerns. The committee's membership included the most important British politicians of the era, most notably John Russell, Robert Peel and Charles Grey (Lord Howick), Thomas Fowell Buxton and other leading abolitionists, as well as others linked to West Indian interests, such as former Attorney-General William Burge, long-time agent for the Jamaican legislature in Britain. The committee said it wished to examine two main points: whether there was a greater danger of rebellion from granting or denying freedom (a serious consideration in the aftermath of the 1831 uprising); and if emancipated, whether former slaves would be industrious.

The Select Committee on the Extinction of Slavery was certainly concerned with evidence about the industriousness of slaves. Witnesses faced question after question seeking assurances of slaves' willingness to work and the extent to which they might be attracted to wage labour if free. Most witnesses reported that slaves were prepared to work hard and well when they perceived it in their own interest to do so, whether this was in hired labour for wages outside of crop time, or most often, in their own provision grounds and home gardens. But witnesses also assured the committee that if ex-slaves were left in the possession of their provision grounds, they would not labour for wages. In a question to John Barry, a Wesleyan minister who had been in Jamaica for eight years, the committee summed up the problem as they perceived it. "Suppose," its chairman asked, "the 300,000 negroes in the island of Jamaica to be in possession of land upon which they are at liberty to labour as long or as short a time as they please, to produce provisions upon that land, which they carry to market and sell at a profit; in such a state of things, what possible inducement could there be for the negro to hire himself to the master for the purpose of labouring at cane hole digging?" Though Barry attempted to assure them that there were "comparatively few of the negroes that could purchase ground" — an erroneous assurance as it turns out — the bulk of the committee was clearly not convinced.[20]

The committee also explored briefly an issue that had become important in political economy arguments after the publication in 1820 of Robert Malthus's *Principles of Political Economy*. In this work, Malthus had partially refuted his famous arguments about the perils of population increase and instead focused on the role of increased needs.[21] The committee termed these "artificial wants" and asked a number of witnesses if it was likely such increased needs could be induced among "negroes." The most common phrasing of the question demonstrated their continued scepticism. When questioning William Taylor, the committee chair defined artificial wants as "any luxuries beyond what is necessary for comfortable food and clothing of the individual" and ended with the leading question: "Is not the negro character such that they do not much look to any thing beyond the necessary comforts of life?" Despite Taylor's assurances that "many of them have a keen relish for the comforts of life," it is clear the committee disagreed.[22] Committee members were reinforced in this image by constant assertions from Jamaica of those who sought either to apologize for slavery or to delay its abolition. James Hakewill, for example, argued in the early 1820s, "Suppose the negro emancipated, what motive would he have for working? ... In a state of liberty, the negro wants little or no clothing; the work of a few hours will supply him with provisions for as many months; and with what more could labour furnish him?"[23]

The result of these various concerns and disputes was the passage of a strange kind of freedom, what William Knibb, a Baptist minister, termed a "land of half freedom."[24] West Indian sugar interests and merchants effectively shaped the nature of emancipation. One favoured scheme, put forward by the Colonial Secretary, would bind slaves to their masters through a twelve-year apprenticeship, during which the slaves would pay for their "value." Buxton was able to have the apprenticeship reduced to six years but only by getting Parliament to approve an additional £20 million compensation to slave owners for their loss of property. For many owners, the compensation simply paid off part of the mortgage. The bulk of the money eventually came to rest among a couple of dozen large merchant houses.[25]

Apprenticeship was, in this context, a state of suspended freedom. All adult slaves were required to stay on the estate of their owner and to work free of wages for 40.5 hours a week. Extra time could be spent working for wages on the estate or elsewhere. Henry Taylor, a fixture in the Colonial Office for decades during the 19th century, had presented the issue to Cabinet by citing the numerous testimonies indicating ex-slaves could meet their necessities by working on the provision lands for one day a week. He asked: "What, except compulsion, shall make them work for six?" For Taylor, the extended period of semi-slavery represented by the apprenticeship would mean ex-slaves "would have acquired habits of self-command and voluntary industry to take with him into freedom, by which habits he would be saved from a life of savage sloth and the planter from ruin."[26] Special magistrates were appointed by London to oversee the apprenticeship process.

Apprenticeship proved to be neither a path to voluntary labour nor to recovery for the sugar economy. Sugar estate owners quite logically sought to drive apprentices as hard as they could, extracting the maximum amount of labour in the limited years they had left to command it. As one ex-slave said, it was like the owners wanted to squeeze all the remaining juice out of the slaves.[27]

The almost inevitable result was an increasingly violent disciplining of labour. Even before the end of slavery, estate owners had often turned to prisons and official workhouses to discipline labour. This continued during the apprenticeship, but as Diana Paton has pointed out, there was a contradiction in the use of prisons as punishment for people who were not free. The only effective remedy was to make the workhouse even more horrific than this brutal apprenticeship. This was accomplished through floggings and other punishments, and with more horrendous work, in the form of chained penal gangs, than even the sugar mill could provide. Those found in violation of their duties as apprentices could be subjected to extra hours of work on the estate at the discretion of the overseer; there was obviously a significant advantage to estates if such punishments were enforced.[28]

After 1834, Jamaican workhouses relied increasingly on a special form of "work": the treadmill,[29] a large cylinder of wood with steps around its circumference. Prisoners' arms were attached to a bar above their heads and they had to keep step as the wheel turned. "Dancing the tread-mill" was brutal punishment. As James Williams, an apprentice brought to England to testify against the apprentice system in the 1830s, stated, "the sweat all run down from them — the steps all wash up with the sweat … the people can't catch the step at all — then the other boatswain flogging away and cutting the people's legs and backs without mercy. The people bawl and cry so dreadful." Williams argued that punishments were more common and more severe under apprenticeship than under slavery. He said he had never experienced it while a slave but had been flogged seven times since the beginning of the apprenticeship period.[30] As Baptist minister James Phillippo argued, the apprentice system "instead of a diminution … was a frightful addition to the miseries of the negro population." He estimated that in the first two years of apprenticeship, 60,000 apprentices received 250,000 lashes and 50,000 were put on the treadmill.[31] He was not alone in his protestations: one special magistrate warned in 1836 that apprentices were being treated so badly that "it will be the means of doing so much injury to the colony that it will become a second St. Domingo [sic]."[32]

Abolitionists and others who had supported the end of slavery were outraged at the violence of the apprentice system. Partly because of their efforts, the Report from the Select Committee on Negro Apprenticeship in the Colonies in 1836 recommended some significant imperial intrusions into the ability of the Jamaican Legislature to pass laws for the island — a right guarded for close to 200 years. Threatened with increased vigilance and control from Britain, the Jamaican Colonial Assembly ended the apprentice system in 1838.

Despite the importance of punishment and the costs of manumission, conflict during the apprentice period most often revolved around two fundamental issues: the amount of work ex-slaves would do, and closely related to that, their ability to control, and work on, their provision grounds. Slaves were required to work 40.5 hours a week without pay under the conditions of their apprenticeship. Still, many estate owners professed to be unable to manage on the labour provided by the apprentice program and were forced to pay wages for some part of their duties. Most complained of the need to pay high wages and the difficulties in getting "continuous and steady" labour from ex-slaves.[33]

One constant source of conflict was the configuration of the work week. Forty and a half hours could be demanded in a variety of ways: the two most common were five roughly equal days of eight hours each or four days of nine hours and a half day on Friday. Apprentices almost unanimously favoured the latter as it gave them time to tend to provision grounds on Friday afternoons. This became especially important as Sunday markets were banned, partly on religious grounds and partly due to protests by traders and retailers concerned about competition from slaves marketing the products of their own provision grounds. Planters often favoured the eight-hour day precisely because it limited apprentices' ability to work on provision grounds and reduced their independence. One special magistrate agreed that the imposition of the eight-hour, five-day rotation was "a great evil to the negroes."[34] Another special magistrate reported that the imposition of the eight-hour system was brought in "for the purpose of punishing the negroes."[35] Conflict continued until the apprentice system was brought to an early end on August 1, 1838.

"The Germ of a Noble Free Peasantry"

The Baptist minister William Knibb, in an 1839 letter commenting on the burgeoning settlement of freeholders who purchased land in his community, celebrated the evidence that, "we have the germ of a noble free peasantry."[36] Not everyone was so thrilled at the prospect. The continuing difficulties of the Jamaican sugar economy, heightened significantly when preferential tariffs were reduced in 1846, were blamed on the unwillingness of freed slaves to provide continuous and steady labour at "reasonable" wages for the estates. Such inattention to the needs of the sugar plantations was equated with indolence, despite constant descriptions of hard work and prosperity on former provision grounds or in freehold estates. As one magistrate in the 1850s argued, "Their march back to barbarism has been rapid and successful."[37] Fortunately, we have different accounts.

Baptist ministers in Jamaica argued that sugar estate owners and managers ensured there would be bitter relations between the ex-slaves and the estates by trying to force them to labour for low wages. Wages during the last few years of the apprentice period had averaged over one shilling a day. This was acceptable to estate owners only because the bulk of the labour was unpaid. With the ending of the apprentice period, owners tried to drive wages below one shilling, but with the encouragement of at least some Baptist ministers, ex-slaves held out for higher wages. For about six months after the August 1, 1838, end of apprenticeship, few labourers reported to the estates and little sugar work was done.[38]

Estate owners and managers attempted to pry more labour from ex-slaves through manipulation of huts, gardens and provision grounds, all long considered slave property. Some forced those who would not work on the estate from their huts and denied them access to provision grounds. In 1839, the Jamaican Assembly passed harsh vagrancy laws, and in 1840, the Ejectment Act allowed for the immediate eviction of those who refused to pay rent on former provision grounds. Others charged higher rents of those who did not labour on the estates or attempted to increase rents dramatically to force ex-slaves to labour.[39] These actions mostly seemed to antagonize ex-slaves and drive them from the estates.

Even before the end of the apprentice period, Baptist ministers were organizing "refuge" communities for those who had bought themselves out of apprenticeship and no longer had access to garden and provision grounds. The first such community, Sligoville, named after the governor, was started in 1835. James Munro Phillippo, one of the Baptists involved in the community, reported that by the early 1840s, many of those who settled without a penny in the community "worked, and paid for the land by its produce. They have erected comfortable cottages, and are now living in perfect happiness, as far as human happiness can be perfect."[40] William Knibb advised ex-slaves in his church to resist attempts to reduce wages, and as the struggle wore on, began to buy up land to establish free communities.[41] By January, 1839, Knibb was excitedly reporting "our little Birmingham is already a refuge for the destitute."[42]

Knibb and the other Baptist ministers stressed that parishioners in these communities were meant to work for wages on neighbouring estates — and the plots of land were kept small to ensure that "our desire being that the cultivation of sugar-cane should proceed, but proceed on righteous principles."[43] He was not always consistent in this approach. In correspondence with other Baptists, he reasoned, "If a few sugar estates are abandoned so much the better, eventually it will be the making of Jamaica. Sugar is sweet, but the liberty of man is much more sweet."[44] Planters soon refused to sell land to the Baptists to prevent the establishment of such communities, compelling Knibb and others to buy through intermediaries. Nonetheless, these free communities multiplied.

Planters were intent on preventing ex-slaves from getting access to land that would provide an alternative to labouring on estates — but they were largely unsuccessful. Hinton Spalding, who owned four coffee estates, had stopped charging rent to those who worked on the estate in a bid to maintain control over labour. He warned the Select Committee and other estate owners that it would not be in their interests to sell land to labourers. He told the committee, "I found my labourers were deserting me to buy land elsewhere ... I told them, 'No, they might as well buy land from me as another.'"[45] Still, he said, once they purchased land, they seldom provided work on his fields. Spalding was not the only owner who, despite recognizing the effect it might have on access to labour, sold parts of his property in small lots to ex-slaves.[46]

Planters recognized that ex-slaves might retreat to the interior. As one planter warned: "If the lands in the interior get into the possession of the Negro, goodbye to lowland cultivation, and to any cultivation."[47] Despite planter and official opposition, ex-slaves left the plantations in droves and established themselves on the land. By the early 1840s, there were more than 150 "free villages" with over 100,000 acres of land; by the middle of that decade, close to 20,000 official landholdings were smaller than ten acres.[48] Though Knibb and many of the other Baptists had stressed that they were locating their communities near estates and expected ex-slaves to continue to provide labour for wages, those fleeing the memory of slavery and the estates were not so easily contained. Denied provision lands they had long used on estates, ex-slaves vigorously sought land elsewhere, mostly in the interior of the country; one planter called this "buying mountains."[49] There was a remarkable migration from the parishes in which cane dominated to the more mountainous interior. In St. Ann, for example, less than two years after the end of apprenticeship, 3000 acres had been bought up in small lots; by 1860, a third of the black population in the island lived in independent villages in the interior.[50] As Philip Curtin argued, "While the planters were struggling with the estates, the Negroes were building a second Jamaica in the hills and building it in their own way."[51]

As in slavery, despite the multiple obstacles placed in their path, such peasant production in the interior proved remarkably productive. Even those who, like Robert Paterson, defended the planters and argued for measures to force labour, reported on the relative comfort provided by the small plots of land farmed by former slaves. More sympathetic observers marvelled at their productivity and industriousness. Although he didn't visit Jamaica, John Davy, the Inspector General of Army Hospitals in the Caribbean, commented on smallholder agriculture in Barbados in the 1850s:

> The culture of these small properties is remarkable…. The crops grown are extremely various, and the produce commonly large…. On one little property … there may be seen growing side by side, or intermixed, almost all the different vegetables which are in request in the island — the sugar cane, yam, sweet-potatoe, eddoe, cassava, ground nut, and in some parts of the island in addition the cotton plant, ginger, arrow root and aloe.

In addition, he reported, they are "rarely without poultry" and have other stock in the form of a cow, a bullock, one or two goats, or sheep, a pig or two.[52]

W. Sewell, an American, admitted that when he first arrived in Jamaica in the 1850s, he came with the idea that emancipation had been a "curse to every branch of agricultural and commercial industry" but instead, "I shall leave these islands overwhelmed with a very opposite conviction." He said the "mountain settlers" he encountered were as "well off as one would wish to see any people in the world." They were, he argued, willing to work for wages when it did not interfere with the necessary labour on their properties even though nine out of ten of them can "rely principally upon their own properties for the support of themselves and their families" and are "about as independent of labor for daily wages as it is possible for any peasantry to be." Sewell also provided various descriptions of the produce of these small plots of land, averaging, in his estimate, three acres; they grew corn, yams, cocoas, plantains, bananas, tobacco, peas, ochro, coffee, pimento, arrow root and even sometimes sugar cane. Even an acre of land, he said, supported a family and allowed them to save money.[53]

There was a chorus of testimony about the productivity, industriousness, and prosperity of the ex-slaves turned peasants in Jamaica after 1838. Lord Elgin stated, after a tour in 1843, that peasants everywhere there "bore a cheerful and willing testimony to the comforts they enjoy"; Governor Metcalfe stated: "I do not suppose that any peasantry in the world have so many comforts, or so much independence or enjoyment"; the Hanover Society of Industry asserted that an acre of land in Hanover Parish could provide for a family's consumption and about £30 worth of marketable crops; and in 1850, John Bigelow described a plot of land of less than two acres that contained "the bread fruit, bananas, yams, oranges, shadducks, cucumbers, beans, pine-apple, plantain and chiramoya, besides many kinds of shrubbery and fruits of secondary value."[54] Jean Besson described these garden lands as "multicropped food forests" producing coconut, breadfruit, plantains, bananas, intensively cropped corn, coconuts, dasheen, Irish and sweet potatoes, cassava, yams, tomatoes, onions, callaloo, capsicums, scallions, beans, peppers, peppermint, thyme. They also supported the raising of chickens, goats, ducks and of course, pigs.[55]

However, many saw this as Jamaica's greatest evil. The Select Committee on the West India Colonies questioned Alexander Geddes, who had been a planter in Jamaica for twenty-two years, and was astonished to learn what a labourer could get from small amounts of land. In response to a leading question from the committee chair, Geddes answered that such lands provided "labourers" in Jamaica with "comforts and luxuries to an extent not known by any peasantry in the world." The committee chair persisted: "And beyond, according to the habits of the rest of the world, what a labouring population could fairly expect?" Geddes responded, "Quite beyond anything I ever heard of."[56]

"Violence to their Nature": Pumpkin Patches and Repression

Indeed, the official strategy for Jamaica soon turned to designing methods to ensure the transition from wage labour to peasant was more difficult and less rewarding; making their returns accord more fully with what they should "fairly expect." This increasingly repressive attitude was in part the result of a racist argument about the inability of "negroes" to cultivate increased need in order to stimulate further industry once some basic needs were met. This had been a major concern of the more mature Robert Malthus, who had argued in his 1820 *Principles of Political Economy* that the key to fostering continued industry among a labouring population was "to inspire them with the wants best calculated to excite their exertions in the production of wealth." In this way, Malthus argued, "It is unquestionably true that wealth produces wants; but it is a still more important truth, that wants produce wealth."[57] Arguments about the unwillingness of Jamaican peasants to provide labour for sugar estates soon focused on these ideas and linked a propensity for such indolence with a racist argument about the inherent character of "negroes."

One can trace this harsher, more racist attitude in various statements about ex-slaves' willingness to work for luxury. In 1833, one member of the British parliament, speaking in support of the apprentice system, argued that ex-slaves "must be gradually taught to desire those objects which could be attained by human labour."[58] By the next decade, the rhetoric was much harsher. In 1849, Thomas Carlyle, the Scottish writer, lecturer and intellectual, had followed up his 1843 paean to discipline and work, *Past and Present*, with an indictment of colonial policy in the West Indies and the misguided attempts at philanthropy in his "Occasional Discourse on the Negro Question." Here he argued that some new form of slavery needed to be imposed on the islands to prevent the ex-slaves from living off the land: "Sitting yonder with their beautiful muzzles up to the ears in pumpkins ... while the sugar-crops rot round them uncut, because labour cannot be hired."[59] Carlyle's work prompted significant debate in England. Catherine Hall says this was the point at which it became acceptable for public men to argue for an "essential inferiority of black people."[60] Though John Stuart Mill and some other notables disputed Carlyle's most egregious arguments, Carlyle's publication provides a convenient marker for the moment when, according to Hall, "The 'good negro' of the abolitionists became the 'nigger' of the mid-Victorian imagination."[61] This "imaginary" figure was increasingly addressed when policy concerning Jamaican peasants was devised.

So, for example, a review of John Bigelow's 1850 book on Jamaica in the *Democratic Review* argued that in Jamaica "a completely savage state is rapidly being approximated" partly because attempting to make "negroes" desire anything but mere subsistence would "do violence to their nature."[62] By 1859, Anthony Trollope's amateurish musings on racial categorization and miscegenation, the intellectual and energetic failings of Blacks and digressions about which Black men, those in Jamaica or those in other

Caribbean colonies, were lazier, seemed almost normal.[63] As the *Times* would argue the next year:

> Floods of pathetic eloquence and long years of parliamentary struggling have taught us to imagine that the world was made for Sambo, and that the sole use of sugar is to sweeten Sambo's existence. The negro is, no doubt, a very amusing and a very amiable fellow, and we ought to wish him well; but he is also a lazy animal, without any foresight, and therefore requiring to be led and compelled.[64]

These arguments became so pervasive in British society in general, and in political economy in particular, that they were soon echoed even by some Baptists, long the most dedicated defenders of ex-slaves. In 1860, Samuel Oughton, a Baptist minister in Jamaica, echoed Carlyle's 1843 ode to the sanctity of labour, arguing, "It is the law of God and Nature, that man should labor." He regretted the movement that allowed ex-slaves to settle on freeholds in the interior and away from the plantations, separating "themselves from all the civilising influences of Society." He ended a story in which a peasant preferred to plant things to eat, rather than roses, with the warning, "This reply contains the germ of one of the secret causes which have led to our declining prosperity. So long as the people of Jamaica limit their desires to the gratification of their mainly animal wants, we shall never possess an active, energetic, and industrious population."[65]

Assured that Jamaican peasants would never develop enough of a taste for luxury to prompt unrelenting industriousness, and driven both by sugar planters' demand for labour and by cotton interests fanaticizing about increased Jamaican cotton,[66] much government policy focused on impoverishing peasant agriculture. The Select Committee had continuously pursued this line of inquiry in 1842, usually expressed as a desire to reduce the apparently excessive prosperity of peasants and draw them into wage labour through targeted taxation. Its interrogation of the former governor of Jamaica, Charles Metcalfe, was most interesting in this regard. The committee asked Metcalfe if it would be "expedient" to "throw an impediment in the way of the accumulation of property" by ex-slaves. Metcalfe, to his credit, argued that it would be unjust to do so. Undeterred, the committee asked Metcalfe if direct legislation compelling labour was acceptable. When he responded that it was not possible, the committee again asked about indirect methods to force ex-slaves turned peasants "to give a greater amount of labour to the planters." Metcalfe refused to condone such methods, again registering his disapproval when the committee chair asked if "financial measures" could be used to keep "a certain proportion of the population in the situation of hired labourers." The hostile questioning continued, with the committee, most often led by Lord Howick, proposing various means to reduce the prosperity and thus the independence of peasants and Metcalfe refusing to support any measures designed to discriminate against small farmers and peasants. Finally, when the committee chair asked if he would support measures to promote a "better understanding between the labourer and the planter," Metcalfe responded: "There appears to me to be a very good understanding even now between the labourer and the planter." Of course, a good understanding did not mean a convergence of interests.[67]

After Metcalfe's departure as governor, all sorts of restrictions were placed in the way of land acquisition specifically and peasant prosperity more generally: vagrancy laws, peddler and trader regulations that made it difficult for peasants to market their own products, Sunday labour and market regulations, a range of taxes and charges that weighed most heavily on ex-slaves attempting to gain access to land and to market their goods, prohibitions against restricting cattle from entering crop land, and finally, laws preventing the sale of land in small lots. Combined, these restrictions made it sufficiently difficult for ex-slaves to get land in freehold that a large percentage simply squatted on land in the interior — most of which was owned by sugar estates but had never been used or had been abandoned. Land held precariously tended to be less carefully farmed. More importantly, by the mid-1850s, the government began systematic efforts to evict squatters, a campaign that gained momentum after the Morant Bay rebellion in 1865.

An extended drought in 1844–1845, a cholera epidemic in the early 1850s, another drought in the 1860s, and the US Civil War, which disrupted supplies and reduced markets due to the general decline in the island's economy, all contributed to a more precarious peasant livelihood. More serious though was official antipathy. Taxes increased in the 1850s, resting heavily on peasants and poorer folk. Large landowners pressed peasants in seemingly minor but vexing ways. For example, the law prevented peasants from taking action against cattle that invaded their fields, yet landowners were allowed to shoot pigs or goats that escaped peasant holdings and entered their property. More seriously, peasants were continuously harassed by local magistrates enforcing regulations that made such small-scale farming more difficult. Philip Curtin has pointed out that in one interior parish, St. Thomas-in-the-East, magistrates had handled 256 cases by 1864; of these, a "Negro" worker or settler was the defendant in 250, a planter in just two.[68] Pressure increased under the last three governors, Charles Grey, Henry

Barkly, and Grey's protégé, Edward Eyre, from 1847–1865. Eyre, when first appointed governor, had asked if the treadmill had ever been officially disallowed as punishment.[69]

These escalating harassments embittered peasants and caused much hardship. As peasants' distress heightened, officials demonstrated a more-than-cavalier attitude. One dispatch to Governor Eyre suggested, "I am not sure that this distress is a bad thing. The idleness of the peasantry needs exemplary punishment."[70] Finally, in 1864 and 1865, peasants pressed Governor Eyre and the Colonial Office for relief. They were supported in these petitions by a Baptist minister, Edward Underhill. In 1864, peasants in the parish at St. Ann had sent a petition to Eyre complaining of the encroachment of cattle and the poor state of the roads. In January 1865, in support, Underhill had directed a letter of complaint to Colonial Secretary Edward Cardwell about increased imprisonment for petty debts, excessive taxation on common goods and a lack of employment. The Colonial Office responded with a letter signed by the Queen but composed primarily by the long-term Colonial Office official and friend of Thomas Carlyle, Henry Taylor. The Queen's letter admonished the petitioners, assuring them that their prosperity "depends ... upon their working for Wages, not uncertainly or capriciously, but steadily and continuously, at the times when their labor is wanted, and for so long as it is wanted."[71] It was as if the last thirty years had not occurred, and ex-slaves were being forced into wage labour once again.

Tension increased; in the midst of which a minor case of trespassing by a poor Black farmer came to the courts in St. Thomas-in-the-East. When he was sentenced, a boisterous crowd in the courtroom called on him to appeal the sentence. The next day, police were beaten back when they arrived to arrest some of those who had disrupted the court. The following day, a crowd arrived at the vestries of Morant Bay to confront the local parish custos (mayor). The situation soon escalated and the custos and some others were killed. The rioters then attacked a few neighbouring estates. The governor, in full fright, declared this to be a "wicked and widespread rebellion" and immediately set out with soldiers and the militia to impose order. The rioters had killed twenty-two people in total. Government retribution led to eighty-five people killed without trial, 354 people executed, and more than 1,000 cottages destroyed. Governor Eyre declared that the retribution "has been so prompt and terrible that is never likely to be forgotten."[72]

Following the Morant Bay rebellion, government policy turned even further against peasant livelihoods. The Colonial Office took full control of the Jamaican Assembly and focused its attention on attracting capital, mostly from the US, to the interior of the island. In the process, the government redoubled its efforts to expel squatters, many of whom had turned abandoned land into productive estates more than two decades before. While focused on ejecting squatters, the government offered attractive leases averaging close to 500 acres each to a few hundred lessees.

Douglas Hall has suggested the period between 1838 and 1865 be considered the "dark age of Jamaican history" because it is ignored in historical writing.[73] Ignored it is, but from the perspective of peasant productivity and prosperity, perhaps it should be considered a golden age.

NOTES

1   British Parliamentary Papers, "Report from the Select Committee on West India Colonies," *House of Commons Papers* (479), 1842, July 25, 1842, 506.

2   *Economist*, "The Deficiency of Labour in the West Indies," 17:829 (July 16, 1859), 784–786.

3   B.W. Higman, *Slave Population and Economy in Jamaica, 1807–1834*, Cambridge: Cambridge University Press, 1976, 61–62.

4   Richard Dunn, *Sugar and Slaves: The Rise of the Planter Class in the English West Indies, 1624–1713*, Chapel Hill: University of North Carolina Press, 1972, 151.

5   Trevor Burnard, *Mastery, Tyranny, and Desire: Thomas Thistlewood and His Slaves in the Anglo-Jamaican World*, Chapel Hill: University of North Carolina Press, 2004; Douglas Hall, *In Miserable Slavery: Thomas Thistlewood in Jamaica, 1750–1786*, Basingstoke: MacMillan, 1989.

6   Bryan Edwards, *The History, Civil and Commercial, of the British Colonies in the West Indies*, 4 Vols, Philadelphia: James Humphreys, 1806, 2, 348.

7   Alexander Barclay, *A Practical View of the Present State of Slavery in the West Indies* (2nd ed.), London: Smith, Elder & Co., 1827, 314.

8   British Parliamentary Papers, "Report of the Select Committee on the Extinction of Slavery throughout the British Dominions" (721) (1831–1832, 25).

9   Sidney Mintz and Douglas Hall, "The Origins of the Jamaican Internal Marketing System," *Yale University Publications in Anthropology* 57 (1970), 18.

10   William Beckford, *A Descriptive Account of the Island of Jamaica*, Vol. 1, London: T. and J. Egerton, 1790, 256.

11   John Bigelow, *Jamaica in 1850: or, the Effects of Sixteen Years of Freedom on a Slave Colony*, Chicago: University of Illinois Press, 2006, 65 (originally published New York, 1851).

12   James Hakewill, *A Picturesque Tour of the Island of Jamaica, from Drawings Made in the Years 1820 and 1821*, London: Hurst and Robinson, 1825, 4. See also Edward Long writing in the 1770s: Long, *The History of Jamaica*, Vol. 2, 105.

13   Barclay, *A Practical View*, 1827, 68.

14   Long, *The History of Jamaica*, 1774, 410–411.

15   British Parliamentary Papers, "Report of the Select Committee on the Extinction of Slavery," 1831–1832, 18.

16   Higman, *Slave Population*, 1976, 14.

17   Gisela Eisner, *Jamaica, 1830–1930: A Study in Economic Growth*, Manchester:

Manchester University Press, 1961, 127.

18 British Parliamentary Papers, "Report of the Select Committee on the Commercial State of the West India Colonies," *House of Commons Papers* 381 (1831–1832), 18.

19 See especially the testimony of Simon Taylor to the British Parliamentary Papers, "Select Committee on the Commercial State of the West Indies Colonies," 1831–1832, 89–90.

20 British Parliamentary Papers, "Select Committee on the Extinction of Slavery," 1831–1832, 118.

21 Malthus, *Principles of Political Economy*, 1989 [1820], 470, 412–413. For a fuller discussion see Jim Handy, *Apostles of Inequality*, 2022.

22 British Parliamentary Papers, "Select Committee on the Extinction of Slavery," 1831–1832, 18–19.

23 Hakewill, *A Picturesque Tour of the Island of Jamaica*, 1825, 6.

24 John Howard Hinton, *Memoir of William Knibb, Missionary in Jamaica*, 2nd edition, Houlston and Stoneman: London, 1849, 243.

25 Kathleen Mary Butler, *The Economics of Emancipation, 1823–1843*, Chapel Hill: University of North Carolina Press, 1995, 23–27, 71–72.

26 See Thomas C. Holt, *The Problem of Freedom: Race, Labor, and Politics in Jamaica and Britain, 1832–1938*, Baltimore: Johns Hopkins University Press, 1992, esp. 43; Tim Barringer, "Land, Labor, Landscape: Views of the Plantation in Victorian Jamaica," 281–321 in Barringer and Wayne Modest (eds.), *Victorian Jamaica*, Durham: Duke University Press, 2018, esp. 287.

27 James Williams, *A Narrative of Events since the First of August, 1834, by James Williams, an Apprenticed Labourer in Jamaica* (edited and with an introduction by Diana Paton), Durham: Duke University Press, 2001 [1837], 5.

28 See for example the testimony of Captain W. Oldrey, a former special magistrate to the parish of St. Elizabeth to the British Parliamentary Papers, "Report from the Select Committee on Negro Apprenticeship in the Colonies," *House of Commons Papers* 560, 1836.

29 Diana Paton, *No Bond but the Law: Punishment, Race, and Gender in Jamaican State Formation, 1780–1870*, Durham: Duke University Press, 2004, 33, 90.

30 Ibid., 11.

31 James M. Phillippo, *Jamaica: Its Past and Present State*, Philadelphia: James M. Campbell & Co., 1843, 69.

32 Oldrey in British Parliamentary Papers, "Report from the Select Committee on Negro Apprenticeship in the Colonies," *House of Commons Papers* 560 (1836), 300.

33 It seems clear that many of their complaints were exaggerated. One special magistrate, Charles Brown, reported that in his district, he only encountered one instance when "negroes" refused to work additional hours for wages. In this instance, the request occurred at the same time as planting season on the provision grounds. Charles Brown in ibid., 498.

34 Robert Madden in ibid., 58; also see the "Introduction to the Report" (iv).

35 Capt. W. Oldrey in ibid., 300.

36 Cited Hinton (ed.), *Memoir of William Knibb*, 1849, 314–315.

37 Cited in Holt, *The Problem with Freedom*, 1992, 167.
38 See the evidence of John Candler, a Quaker, before the Select Committee on West India Colonies (British Parliamentary Papers, 1842, 535).
39 See the testimony of Samuel Gooding Barrett to ibid., 1842, 374–375.
40 Phillippo, *Jamaica: Its Past and Present State*, 1843, 86.
41 See Hinton, *Memoir*, 1849, 288–294, and Knibb to Select Committee (British Parliamentary Papers 1842), 421.
42 Knibb to Sturge, January 1839, in Hinton, *Memoir*, 1849, 311–312.
43 Knibb in British Parliamentary Papers, "Report from the Select Committee on West India Colonies," *House of Commons Papers*, 1842, 423.
44 Knibb to Sturges, January 1839, in Hinton, *Memoir*, 1849, 312.
45 British Parliamentary Papers, "Report from the Select Committee," 1842, 404–405.
46 See Henry Lowndes in British Parliamentary Papers, "Report from the Select Committee," 1842, 366.
47 Cited in Hall, *Free Jamaica*, New Haven: Yale University Press, 1959, 21.
48 Eisner, *Jamaica, 1830–1930*, 1961, 210–212.
49 William Taylor in British Parliamentary Papers, "Select Committee on the Extinction of Slavery," 1831–1832, 17.
50 Barringer, "Land, Labor, Landscape," 2018, 294; Eisner, *Jamaica, 1830–1930*, 1961, 185; Hall, *Free Jamaica*, 1959, 25.
51 Philip Curtin, *Two Jamaicas: The Role of Ideas in a Tropical Colony, 1830–1865*, New York: Greenwood Press, 1968, 157.
52 Davy, *The West Indies*, 1854, 149–151.
53 W.G. Sewell, *The Ordeal of Free Labour in the British West Indies*, New York: Harper and Brothers, 1861, esp. 177, 188, 201–202, 247–249, 251.
54 See Hall, *Free Jamaica*, 1959, 27; Eisner, *Jamaica, 1830–1930*, 1961, 212, 217; Bigelow, *Jamaica in 1850*, 2006, 116.
55 Jean Besson, *Martha Brae's Two Histories: European Expansion and Caribbean Culture-Building in Jamaica*, Chapel Hill: University of North Carolina Press, 2002, 197–198; Curtin, *Two Jamaicas,*, 1968, 19. See also the well-known arguments of the cultural geographer Carl Sauer, who in the 1950s argued that Caribbean garden agriculture, the *conuco*, was a "many-storied cultural vegetation, producing at all levels, from tubers underground through understory of pigeon peas and coffee, a second story of cacao and bananas, to a canopy of fruit trees and palms … its messy appearance … meaning that all the niches are properly filled."
56 British Parliamentary Papers, "Select Committee," 1842, 472.
57 Malthus, *Principles of Political Economy*, 1989, [1820] 470–472.
58 Cited in Holt, *The Problem*, 1992, 54.
59 Thomas Carlyle, *Occasional Discourse on the Nigger Question*, London: Thomas Bosworth, 1853, esp. 5. Note the 1853 pamphlet was entitled *Occasional Discourse on the Nigger Question*. It was first published in *Fraser Magazine* (Dec. 1849) as "Occasional Discourse on the Negro Question."
60 Catherine Hall, *Civilising Subjects: Metropole and Colony in the English Imagination, 1830–1867*, Chicago: University of Chicago Press, 2002, 48.

61 Ibid., 25.

62 Cited in Robert Scholnick's introduction to the 2006 edition of Bigelow's book, xlii.

63 Anthony Trollope, *The West Indies and the Spanish Main,* London: Chapman & Hall, 1859, esp. 74–76, 124.

64 *Times,* Jan. 6, 1860, also cited in Hall, *Civilising,* 2002, 216.

65 Samuel Oughton, "The Influence of Artificial Wants on the Social, Moral and Commercial Advancement of Jamaica," *West India Quarterly,* June 1862, reprinted in Oughton, *Roupell the Forger, the Lessons of His Crime and Punishment,* Kingston: DeCordova, McDougall and Co., 1862, 474–482, esp. 476, 480.

66 For a further discussion of cotton dreams, see Handy, *Apostles of Inequality,* 2022, ch. 11.

67 British Parliamentary Papers, "Report from the Select Committee," 1842, 512–524.

68 Curtin, *Two Jamaicas,* 1968, 130, 194.

69 Hall, *Civilising,* 2002, 59.

70 Cited in Hall, *Free Jamaica,* 1959, 244.

71 Underhill's petition and the Queen's letter are included in Edward Bean Underhill, *A Letter Addressed to the Rt. Honourable E. Cardwell,* London: Arthur Miall, 1865: the Queen's advice, 5–6; Eyre, 6; Underhill to Cardwell, 10–16; Catherine Hall makes the case that this was composed by Henry Taylor and includes the St. Ann petition, *Civilising,* 2002, 244–245.

72 Cited in Hall, *Free Jamaica,* 1959, 248. The fullest description of the events surrounding Morant Bay is presented in Gad Heuman, *The Killing Time: The Morant Bay Rebellion in Jamaica,* Knoxville: University of Tennessee Press, 1994; see also Mimi Sheller, *Democracy after Slavery: Black Publics and Peasant Radicalism in Haiti and Jamaica,* Gainesville: University Press of Florida, 2000, esp. 198–246.

73 Hall, *Free Jamaica,* 1959, vii.

4 Guatemala: They Flattened Our Milpa

In 1982, the Guatemalan military entered the Achi Mayan village of Plan de Sánchez in the Department of Baja Verapaz. According to testimony from villagers collected by the Human Rights Office of the Archbishopric of Guatemala, the military "destroyed our houses, stole our goods, burned our clothes, took away our animals, flattened our milpa, they hunted us day and night." A little farther north and a couple of years later, Ixil villagers from Santa Clara, Chajul, Quiché, reported that they had initially fled to the area around Santa Clara when their villages were attacked. In their new homes, they "began to sow maiz, malango, caña, [but] we were always hunted and when the military entered, they cut everything and burned the houses."[1]

In the context of the horrific violence in Guatemala in the 1980s, these reports were not particularly shocking. Since the overthrow of the government of Jacobo Arbenz in 1954, Guatemala had been convulsed by ever-increasing state-led violence; in the late 1970s and early 1980s this violence reached nightmarish levels. The Commission for the Clarification of History created by the United Nations reported that more than 200,000 people were killed, 93 percent victims of the military or its agents, and that during the worst of the violence, 83 percent of the victims were Mayan. The commission asserted that the military had engaged in genocidal acts and that "the massacres, scorched earth operations, forced disappearances and executions of Mayan authorities, leaders, and spiritual guides, were not only an attempt to destroy the social base of the guerrillas, but above all, to destroy the cultural values that ensured cohesion and collective action in Mayan communities." Nonetheless, the commission also focused on issues of social and economic inequality in explaining the violence; the state became an instrument for the protection of a "system of multiple exclusions."[2]

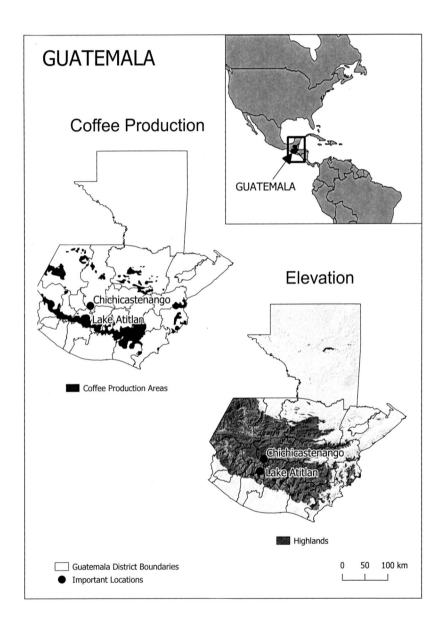

GUATEMALA

Coffee Production

Chichicastenango
Lake Atitlan

■ Coffee Production Areas

Elevation

Chichicastenango
Lake Atitlan

■ Highlands

□ Guatemala District Boundaries
● Important Locations

0   50   100 km

All of this is reasonably well known; the two reports mentioned above have been widely cited and disseminated. A number of academic and activist books and reports outlined the scope of the violence while it was occurring; even more have since attempted to analyze and explain it. Like the Commission for the Clarification of History, many have focused either on the racial aspects of continuing violence — that is, the genocidal and systemic violence against Indigenous people in Guatemala — or the economic dimensions of the violence — that is, the use of the state to maintain this "system of multiple exclusions."[3] Both of these approaches are useful, especially as they converge and the racist and exclusionary nature of the Guatemalan state and economy is revealed. But the testimony of survivors also demonstrated how often these attacks focused on the bases of peasant livelihoods: they "flattened our milpa, burned our fields, stole our animals, destroyed our seeds and prevented us from working in our fields" emerges as the central motif on virtually every page.

Violence against peasants is not restricted to a particularly devastating moment in Guatemala's past; rather it permeates the country's entire history. This violence was accompanied, and often excused, by a discourse that linked the perceived poverty of Mayan villages to supposed inherent defects in Mayan culture and to the race itself. Like those identified for Jamaican ex-slaves, these supposed defects were perceived to require often brutal initiations into the wonders of wage labour. Yet there is plenty of evidence for the productivity and industriousness of Mayan peasants in Guatemala through the 19th and 20th centuries. They integrated a multitude of crops in very small landholdings in difficult terrain and often obtained remarkable yields. Instead of attacking peasant livelihoods to extract labour for export agriculture or in the name of agricultural efficiency, recognizing that productivity might well have led to a nation distinguished by sustained and equitable development — rather than one marked by constant violence, widespread poverty and deep-seated racial tension. This chapter focuses on the history of state-led or state-abetted violence against and dispossession of Mayan peasants in Guatemala. It contrasts the rhetoric used to justify that violence with evidence of the productivity and innovation demonstrated by Mayan peasant cultivators.

Milpa and Belonging

Guatemalan Mayan peasant agriculture in the 19th century emerged out of the cataclysmic collapse of population following the Spanish conquest (1524–1667) and subsequent centuries of epidemic diseases. From the middle of the 16th century to the middle of the 18th century, the Mayan population of Guatemala declined by 90–95 percent.[4] Coming in the slipstream of conquest and colonial rule, this collapse not only devastated cultural traditions and political allegiances but also fundamentally challenged native agricultural systems. Intensive agriculture, such as that followed in both highland and lowland Guatemala in the pre-conquest period, required lots of labour. Population loss coupled with Spanish demands for labour and tribute fundamentally disrupted complex agricultural practices.[5]

Mayan population levels did not begin to recover until the 18th century and then did so only slowly. Core peasant livelihoods revolved around *milpa*, a complex agricultural system usually intercropping maize, beans, squash and herbs, now augmented by imported domesticated animals such as sheep in the highest reaches, pigs and fowl in peasant households. However, Indigenous communities also took advantage of the increased availability of land, especially in the Pacific lowlands, where Indigenous populations had been hit even harder by disease. Land in the Pacific lowlands and piedmont was used both for maize production — in some regions two crops could be taken each year — and for a wide range of distinct annual and permaculture agricultural pursuits. Highland communities used new land to augment core *milpa* production, diversify subsistence and produce crops for the market.[6]

However, by the second half of the 19th century, Indigenous peasants in Guatemala were subject to intense pressures. Even before coffee cultivation had made much of an impact on the country, the government of Rafael Carrera showed increased interest in fostering agricultural export production. It used the instruments of a modern state to begin to classify citizens and land in ways meant to assist this production. Early attempts at a census sought to count and distinguish inhabitants by race — Indigenous or non-Indigenous (Ladino) — and began the process of cementing what until then had been a more fluid identity. Without clear and definitive markers, census-takers used a range of characteristics to help in this classification; language and dress were common. More devastatingly, however, census-takers also applied perceptions of poverty and attempted to distinguish identity based on agricultural pursuits.[7]

At roughly the same time, land-use surveys began to be used extensively, driven by many of the same impulses. In many areas, surveyors were told to ignore land in *milpa* and only provide detailed surveys (and thus ascribe ownership) to land planted in other, single crops. Perhaps inevitably, the preconceptions inherent in both these state instruments converged, and one characteristic used to distinguish Maya from Ladino was whether they grew *milpa* or not. As a result, land in the hands of Mayan peasants was most often not surveyed. It was given a kind of generalized and indistinct patrimony, often lumped together on survey maps as *milpero*, of little interest to the state and with questionable ownership. The assumption was that agriculture undertaken in multicropped locations not dedicated to the production of a single, marketable, preferably exportable commodity was "traditional," demonstrating little capacity for innovation. Land in specific marketable crops such as cochineal and, increasingly, coffee for export, was often carefully delineated and assigned owners. Increasingly, these owners were assumed to be Ladino.[8]

Nonetheless, until the 1860s, Guatemalan governments under the influence of Rafael Carrera were limited in the ways they could facilitate export agricultural production if it meant either forcing labour or appropriating land from Mayan peasant communities. The Carrera administrations were aware of the importance of Mayan peasants as producers of the bulk of the country's foodstuffs and were thus leery of the potential for revolt, especially as Carrera relied heavily on community militias.[9]

The Coffee Revolution

Government policy turned against peasants in the latter part of the 19th century. Cochineal, which had been the most important export crop through the middle of the 19th century, had depended mostly on small-scale producers. Guatemalan elite most often made profits from cochineal through marketing arrangements.[10] Historians at one time suggested that cochineal production was mostly the preserve of Mayan peasants. This appears not to have been the case, as both small and larger Ladino producers in the Panchoy Valley, around Lake Amatitlán, and the predominantly Ladino Oriente, produced the bulk of the crop. When coffee began to be grown in quantity in Guatemala, it followed a similar pattern. Indeed, in many instances in the Panchoy Valley, it was simply substituted for cochineal.[11]

Coffee can work sympathetically with peasant production: there are few economies of scale, good Arabica coffee requires a carefully maintained shade canopy — various productive trees can be used for such shade, providing both foodstuffs and biomass for fuel — and coffee itself can be grown along with a range of understory plants. In addition, coffee requires a significant amount of skilled labour for a few months each year during harvest, which in Guatemala runs from November to January. Good Arabica coffee needs to be picked when ripe; coffee cherries ripen at uneven rates, thus requiring harvest by experienced hands. Before the spread of "technified," full-sun coffee after the 1970s, there was little opportunity for mechanical interventions to reduce labour demands. In addition, the technology for the initial processing of coffee — that is, husking and drying — remained relatively simple and inexpensive almost until the end of the 20th century. All of this meant that coffee could be produced by peasant households and contribute substantially to peasant well-being.

In Guatemala, many Mayan peasants engaged in coffee production in the early years of its expansion. They seemed to have enjoyed success similar to small-scale coffee producers elsewhere. Their ability to compete was augmented by the flexibility of their agriculture. Long-term planning and significant investment are required during the wait for coffee trees to produce; peasant labour can turn to *milpa* and other agricultural pursuits in the interim and can concentrate labour efforts elsewhere when the price of coffee doesn't compare favourably with other products. This seems to have played a part in the significant increase in *milpa* production as coffee prices collapsed in the first few years of the 1930s depression.[12]

Although some Mayan communities were still able to combine coffee and *milpa*, such small-scale production was eventually swamped by large estate-holders employing significant, coerced and badly paid Mayan labour.[13] Coffee production in Guatemala developed through a particularly rapacious capitalist regime that devastated peasant livelihoods, impoverished Mayan villages and cemented a racist discourse that had horrendous consequences. Guatemalan Mayan peasants were quite prepared to take advantage of the opportunities provided by coffee when first presented with them. But production didn't increase fast enough to satisfy government officials, and the constraints on the accumulation of capital and the development of large-scale coffee estates — a shortage of available labour at cheap rates, community restraints on the accumulation of land by outsiders, difficulties in marshalling capital because of the lack of financing based on land values — frustrated landholding elites in western Guatemala. In collaboration with Liberals elsewhere in the country, these elites mounted a revolution. In power, they unleashed a series of reforms meant to favour large-scale coffee production by freeing land and labour for coffee. In the process, they devastated peasant livelihoods.

Large-scale commercial coffee production required land. Its accumulation appears to have happened in diverse and sometimes piecemeal ways before the Liberal Revolution in 1871: through individual titling by outsiders of land held by Indigenous communities (especially land not in the core highland community and therefore less carefully controlled by custom) and often through the mechanism of the *censo enfitéutico* — the right to lease land in exchange for a small rent. The tendency for government surveyors to register land used for "commercial" crops and to assign an owner, often assumed to be Ladino, while not registering ownership of land in *milpa*, no doubt also contributed to the ease with which this occurred.[14] After 1871 and the Liberal reforms, land was taken by military and other elites on a much broader scale, often by declaring community land as *baldío* (empty or waste) to be auctioned or allocated in other ways by the state. David McCreery, in an important study of land dispossession in Guatemala during this period, indicated that communities at elevations too high for coffee cultivation seldom lost core community land. And a few Indigenous communities, like Santiago Atitlán, were able to use favourable locations, government connections and newly invigorated community customs to augment community resources through the titling of land near the coast, in the "hot" zone. However, many communities in areas where coffee could be grown were engulfed by it.[15] Others lost access to land that had been used to extend and diversify peasant production. Indeed, one geographer described this attack on community-controlled land in the late 19th century as a "second conquest."[16]

Liberal labour regimes did even more to impoverish Indigenous communities. All those involved in coffee production in Guatemala understood the need to have sufficient workers for the harvest. But coffee production began during a point in the demographic recovery of Indigenous population levels when labour in Guatemala was a scarce commodity, as it had been through the colonial period. Moreover, even with the loss of some land, Indigenous peasant households had both limited needs and independent means for survival. Getting sufficient labour for the coffee harvest thus became the all-encompassing obsession for those who had invested capital in it. As one German planter in Alta Verapaz warned in 1886, getting sufficient labour was "a matter of life and death for the planters" but the Indians "despise working on the fincas" and thus "should the government cease to help agriculturalists in securing labourers, the cultivation of coffee would become an impossibility." Another suggested, "Not the soil but rather the low wages of our laborers are the wealth of the Cobán."[17] Indigenous peasants were compelled to provide labour in various ways, from forced labour through the *mandamiento* (an old colonial institution of obligatory labour), to debt bondage abetted by rum, to vagrancy laws.[18] As one local government official declared in 1872, force was necessary because of the "disgraceful condition of the race."[19]

Forced or coerced labour helped impoverish peasant agriculture. In 1903, peasant producers in El Cubo complained, "The mandamiento has ... left our families desolate and destitute ... our agriculture has suffered a great setback."[20] David McCreery argued that forced labour represented a "massive transfer of surplus … to the export economy." Robert Carmack estimated that forced labour provided by the municipality of Momostenango to plantations and public works amounted to approximately 336,000 days per year.[21] In the first few decades of the 20th century, official labour recruitment was replaced by debt bondage abetted by alcohol production. One archaeologist working in the highlands in 1912 reported, "The rum business and the coffee business work together in this country, automatically. The plantation advances money to the Indian and the rum seller takes it away from him and the Indian has to go to work again. Work leads to rum, and rum leads to work."[22] The British attaché to Guatemala described the process:

> From a creditor's point of view, the system is perfectly simple, and nothing but the inconvenient possession of a conscience can stand in the way of the quite indefinite furthering of his own interests. He has only to charge the cost of the unfortunate peon's living at a price that will prevent the man from ever getting out of debt … By this means he secures the lifelong labour of the man, and frequently his children as well. [23]

By the 1920s, a significant percentage of men in almost all highland villages were forced by debt to labour for months on the coffee harvest.[24] Soon deadlier and more onerous work would augment these demands.

Despite or perhaps because of this coercion, the reluctance to labour for wages and determinedly limited needs became the focal point in discussions of problems with "race" in Guatemala. One German immigrant to the country, Fredrich Endler, a mechanic who worked on the La Libertad coffee finca owned by former president Manuel Barillas, complained: "An enormous disadvantage for this country is that the Indians won't work more than enough to fill their basic needs, and those are very few."[25] In an essay in a major newspaper in the 1890s, Ignacio Solis argued that, "to civilize the indigenous population which still remains in a semi-savage state is a double-necessity for the country. It cannot occupy its rightful place among the advanced nations, nor realize fully its industrial, economic, social, and political transformation, while the last vestiges of barbarity remain on its soil."[26] A few years later, the official newspaper argued:

> The Indian is a pariah, stretched out in his hammock and drunk on chichi, his natural beverage. His house is a pig sty; a ragged wife and six or more naked children live beneath a ceiling grimy

with the smoke of a fire that burns day and night in the middle of the floor; some images of saints with the faces of demons, four chickens and a rooster and two or three skinny dogs. Yet in this state the Indian is happy.[27]

Politicians and those most in need of badly paid labour used these tropes to justify continued measures to force labour from Indigenous communities and to blame their poverty — the result of dispossession of land and labour from these communities — on Indigenous peasants themselves.

The Bells Ring in Chichicastenango

Even well into the 20th century, politicians, historians and anthropologists continued to insist that Mayan agricultural techniques were, like much of the culture itself, inflexible and badly adapted to the modern world. In the 1930s, the dictator Jorge Ubico replaced debt bondage with a vagrancy law as the dominant means to force labour from Mayan peasants. The primary result of the change was to increase government control over labour, and thus over coffee *finqueros*, rather than to free Mayan peasants from coerced labour. Ubico sought to augment food production in the country, not by reducing such labour demands but by introducing waves of agricultural experts whose mission was to eliminate "customs and superstitious beliefs … which have hindered our agricultural evolution."[28]

However, foreign observers did not necessarily see peasant production more clearly. In 1940, for example, in what became the "standard" English language history of Guatemala for many decades, Chester Lloyd Jones criticized "Indian cultivators'" unwillingness to produce for the market or to in other ways contribute to a national economy "retarded by the traditional habits of life of the producers."[29] He argued, for example, that Mayan cultivators did not engage in seed selection in cultivating maize, depending instead on unimproved traditional varieties.

More reliable and informed discussions of Indigenous highland agriculture provide a different vision of Mayan agriculture. Even during the most feverish period in the expansion of the coffee regime, near the end of the 19th century, many commentators identified Mayan, peasant involvement in the production of cochineal and coffee. Others were struck by how successfully various highland communities concentrated on producing distinct, specialized crops for the market.[30]

From the 1930s through the 1960s, both North American and Guatemalan anthropologists frequently studied highland Guatemalan

Mayan. These anthropologists were usually most interested in "rediscovering" traditional pre-conquest Mayan beliefs through observations of contemporary Mayan customs. This became known as "salvage" anthropology. Many were unable to accept that they were observing innovation and adaptation rather than centuries-old practices, or to throw off prejudices about peasant agriculture. Nonetheless, their studies sometimes include keen observations about the productivity of peasant agriculture, the hard work this entailed and the deep satisfaction it brought to Mayan highland peasants.

One of the first and most interesting of these anthropologists was Ruth Bunzel, who did field work around Chichicastenango and Sololá in highland Guatemala in the early 1930s. She described Maya and Ladinos living "in a state of polite antagonism, despising one another heartily." Mayan peasants felt Ladinos who did not cultivate land lived a "sordid, insecure and vicious" existence, hounded by debts brought on in part by expanded needs that increased expenditures.[31] She provided a searing and evocative description of the depredations and impoverishment involved in debt bondage, stating that if the worker "is fortunate enough to escape malaria and dysentery ... he is sent back to his mountains ... in debt." And she describes how during the coffee harvest, "every few days the bell in Chichicastenango is tolled to commemorate the passing of some citizen who has died 'in the *finca*.' The bodies are not brought back, but word of the death is sent to relatives who pay to have the bell rung."[32]

Despite these afflictions, Bunzel described the agricultural life of the Kaqchikel Maya around Chichicastenango as one of abundance produced by hard work and productive agriculture. The market was a place of constant bustle as Indian producers from all over the highlands came to trade their goods and to socialize. The homes near town had "carefully tended and irrigated gardens where luscious vegetables are grown the year round." Homes higher in the surrounding hills were "substantial homesteads of adobe and tile .... The whole country wears an air of amplitude and prosperity." There was, inevitably, some conflict between families and across generations over land but there were also deeply observed proscriptions against selling land to anyone outside of the community. The woodlands surrounding the community were carefully maintained "from which generations have been carefully cutting firewood."[33]

The peasant economy and household revolved around corn but agricultural production was extremely diverse. In contrast to Jones' argument above, there were thousands of different varieties of maize in use in Guatemala, the vast majority the result of intensive cross-pollination and plant selection by peasants working to find the best possible corn variety for specific purposes and specific micro-climates.[34] In Chichicastenango, various varieties of corn were planted in different fields, most often with two distinct kinds of beans, either *frijol de milpa*, which winds up the corn stalk or *frijol de surca*, a smaller variety planted between the rows of corn. Most often *milpa* included one or two types of squash, *guisquil* or *chilacayotes*. The list of other vegetables grown on such land is almost endless: along with those already mentioned, peasants in the community grew cabbage, turnips, potatoes, Swiss chard, peach, quince, guava and avocado. Most households kept at least one pig and some chickens, and those in the higher reaches kept sheep. Bunzel described how one small farm of twenty-two *cuerdas* (less than three acres) produced almost all a family needed and a marketable surplus. Bunzel argued that in general in Chichicastenango during her visit from 1930–1932, food was "cheap and plentiful" and rarely would anyone go hungry.[35]

This exceptional productivity was the result not only of a remarkably diverse and carefully constructed agricultural system but also of hard work. In sharp contrast to the newspaper's description provided above and the prevailing attitude in Guatemala that the Maya were lazy, Bunzel says, "the Indian takes no siesta; from the moment of his early rising before dawn has whitened the sky until he extinguishes his *ocote* torch late at night, his day is filled with orderly and unceasing activity …. Except at fiestas I have never seen an idle Indian, male or female."[36]

Though Bunzel was a well-respected anthropologist by the time of her field study in Guatemala, one might be tempted to dismiss her relatively benign view of Mayan peasant agriculture as that of an ill-informed observer, one restricted to a well-situated locale or favourable harvest. Yet many other anthropologists came to similar, if less fulsome, conclusions. When the two renowned anthropologists Sol Tax and Robert Redfield spent some time together in eastern Guatemala and around Chichicastenango in the 1930s and early 1940s, they seemed obsessed by two issues: determining whether those they encountered were truly Maya and finding food they could recognize, eat and store, especially eggs. Tax quipped that their obsession meant, "I'm afraid that … all we shall be able to talk about will be tortillas." Tax particularly depended on the large supply of canned goods he brought along with him, asserting "We have learned that it is seldom possible to live off the country and remain healthy enough to work." Though, when the Guatemalan anthropologist Juan de Díos Rosales accompanied them, he refused the canned goods and apparently survived quite well on the food available.[37]

But other anthropological accounts of peasant lifestyles reflected abundance not entirely different from that portrayed by Bunzel. The Guatemalan anthropologist Antonio Goubaud Carrera, Tax and Díos Rosales did a tour a few years later of northern Guatemala. They noted that even in the cold, high Cuchumatán mountain region, abundant potato and corn crops — maintained partly through intensive use of natural fertilizers — and peasant handicraft production — based on wool from their own sheep — contributed to peasant self-sufficiency and provided significant goods for the market. The anthropologists frequently commented on the abundance of pigs and on the variety of crops grown in distinct locales for sale. Of course, such abundance was not universal; in communities where much of the land had been claimed by Ladinos, the anthropologists perceived more poverty. In San Martín, Huehuetenango, Goubaud reported that Ladinos' fincas dominated the landscape while most peasants had little to no land and needed to go to the coast each year to work: "and the people talk about their poverty as contrasted with the wealth of other towns."[38]

In the more favourable climates around Lake Atitlán, even Sol Tax found lots of evidence of peasant plenty. In the towns surrounding the lake, peasant producers not only had considerable land for *milpa* production for their own consumption but also sold abundant and distinct goods in markets as far away as Guatemala City. Coffee, anise, maguey, a wide range of vegetables and fruit, including jocote and oranges, and a host of other crops were produced in quantity to augment *milpa* and resources from the lake. As Tax argued, "One point is clear … the Indians consciously try to get as much from the soil as possible, in a definition that includes long-term considerations."[39]

Peasants and the Revolution

These reports from the early 1940s were written on the cusp of dramatic political change in Guatemala. In 1944, students, workers and young military cadets overthrew the last remnants of the Liberal regimes that had held sway since the 1870s. They embarked on a series of political, social and economic reforms before the second "revolutionary" administration was overthrown in 1954.

The reform administrations' attitudes to peasant agriculture and livelihoods were complicated and at times contradictory. The major challenge might have seemed obvious. In a country where more than half the population relied on agriculture for a living, 88 percent of landowners had access to less than 14 percent of the agricultural land in the country. In addition, over half of the farms were under three acres in size. Though there were numerous Ladino peasants, especially in the Oriente (or eastern regions of the country), there were also clear racial divisions in land tenure. Nationally, Ladino farmers controlled on average close to 60 acres each, while Mayan farmers controlled on average less than 7.5 acres. In the Western highlands of the country where the majority of the Mayan peasants lived, Ladinos made up 12 percent of the population but controlled 66 percent of the land.[40] Along with such inequality, the country was plagued by its dependence on one or two agricultural exports — coffee, and by the early 20th century, bananas — and by fluctuating prices. It also suffered from periodic shortages in corn, its major food staple.

Despite the apparent link between centuries of land and labour dispossession and peasant poverty, agricultural modernizers in Guatemala, both before and through the early years of the revolutionary decade, seemed to do their best to ignore the connection. Before 1944, periodic corn shortages most often led to exhortations to modernize corn varieties by adopting hybrid seeds and to produce more corn in large, industrial-type agricultural enterprises outside of the highlands. These approaches ignored both the constant innovation and diversification of corn varieties that had been occurring for centuries in Guatemala and the fact that corn cultivation was most often intercropped in intensely productive ways that were not adaptable to such industrialization.[41]

Revolutionary agricultural specialists initially adopted a similar approach to increasing agricultural production. Debates in the Constitutional Assembly, which met in 1944 and 1945 to create a new constitution, often echoed existing arguments about the laziness of Indians and their obstinate unwillingness to work for wages. They warned that agriculture would come to an end in the country if Indians were not compelled to work on the fincas. Notably, however, others sprang to their defence, saying that "if anyone works in this country ... it is peasants." And the constitution removed the worst aspects of the vagrancy law that had compelled Indigenous labour since 1934.[42]

Guatemalan reformers were initially swayed by reports, primarily from North American technical advisors and agronomists, that indiscriminately linked swidden agriculture observed in relatively lightly populated and heavily forested regions of northern Guatemalan with highland *milpa* agriculture, or that warned constantly about the dangers of population increase and soil erosion. Hector Sierra, the Director General of Agriculture for much of the first administration of the revolution, was especially disparaging about Mayan agriculture. Though he recognized peasants' hard work, he argued that the "Guatemalan Indian does not even bother about where or how he plants his corn, his chief object being to have corn planted that he can take care of as tenderly as a father cares for his children." He blamed Guatemala's "low" corn yields compared to those in the US on this adherence to tradition. And although he would protest the comparison, in a description not unlike the one cited earlier from the official newspaper in the late 19th century, Sierra said, "The Indian is happy when he grows corn, even though what he calls happiness is to us misery."[43]

When agricultural extension agents stopped portraying all Mayan peasant agriculture as destructive and focused instead on providing them with appropriate assistance, they found to their surprise that Maya peasants were eager participants in agricultural programs. The most perceptive of these agents soon identified the major obstacles facing Guatemalan agriculture: the combination of land shortage created through inequitable land distribution, constant demands for essentially unpaid labour and the resultant poverty among much of the country's Mayan population. This situation required more drastic remedies.

At first, government agricultural advisors focused on half-steps, primarily three laws, in 1946, 1949 and 1951, that attempted to regulate land rental to peasants. This timid approach reflected the views of the first president during the revolutionary decade, Juan José Arévalo, and the continued influence of the conservative head of the military, Francisco Arana, until his death in 1949. However, by the early 1950s, progressive sectors in the new government of Jacobo Arbenz Guzmán had convinced the president that substantial redistribution of land, from large landowners to peasants, was necessary both to relieve rural poverty and to solidify political support for the revolution. Consequently, in June 1952, that government issued Decree 900, an agrarian reform that Arbenz described as "the most precious fruit of the revolution."[44]

Arbenz and most of those active in his administration demonstrated their sincere commitment to bettering the lives of the rural poor. In his address to the Guatemalan Congress in 1953, Arbenz described them as "the humble people ... with cheap cotton shirts, and palm-leaf sombreros who do not have shoes, or medicine, or money, or education, or land." Nonetheless, their vision of what peasants needed and what Decree 900 would bring was in many ways familiar: agrarian reform and the technical agencies associated with it would transform peasants into small-scale modern farmers who would produce for both the internal market and for export, growing hybrid corn and cotton on the south coast. Some of these advisors also argued that such modernization would reduce food costs and thereby "free" peasants to become wage labourers on plantations and in industry.[45]

Within two years, however, before the Arbenz administration was overthrown in 1954, the government expropriated almost a million acres and provided land to close to 100,000 rural families. This benefitted perhaps 500,000 people out of a population of close to three million. A sixth of the government's total budget was dedicated to agricultural loans given out mostly to small farmers. The result, in terms of overall agricultural production, was impressive. Despite disruption as the reform continued to unfold across the countryside, both coffee and corn harvests increased substantially in 1953 and 1954.[46]

Not surprisingly, however, those who benefited most from the reform did not share entirely the vision espoused by Arbenz and his advisors. The reform was designed to take land from large landowners who were not using the land productively and to distribute it, mostly in lifelong usufruct, to individuals and their families who would be supported by government technical advisors and loans. In practice, it was the actions of Guatemalan peasants that made the reform truly revolutionary. The pace of the reform was dictated by organized peasants who continuously pushed the government to act more quickly. While much of the expropriation of land and its distribution adhered to the terms of Decree 900, peasants clearly saw land in the historical context of long-standing community disputes with neighbouring landowners, and occasionally, with neighbouring communities. Though the law did not stipulate that historic community claims to land would be taken into consideration in expropriation and distribution, such claims formed important parts in the majority of official petitions for land by peasants.[47] The law could not so easily divorce itself from peasant concepts of justice. In addition, when peasants got land through the agrarian reform, at least in the brief period before it was taken from them following the coup, they most often recreated vibrant peasant agricultural pursuits. They planted *milpa* and diverse other annual crops, invested in permaculture and inhabited their farms with chickens and pigs. Peasant livelihoods were not displaced by the reform; rather they were enhanced through access to new land and small amounts of capital. The results appear to have been dramatically beneficial in the brief period before everything fell apart in the coup of 1954.

The Liberación: Eating Cotton

On June 27, 1954, President Arbenz announced on Guatemalan radio that he was resigning in the face of an invasion of counter-revolutionary forces from Honduras — planned and supported by the CIA and the US State

Department — bombing missions flown out of Nicaragua by US pilots, and the opposition to his government by much of the Guatemalan army. With Arbenz's ouster, the revolution quickly came to an end. The self-styled "liberation" government that followed quickly undid all of the democratic reforms initiated during the revolution; primary among these was the agrarian reform. On paper, the Liberation government accepted all the "legal" decisions made under Decree 900. However, it allowed landowners to petition to have land returned to them if the provisions of the decree had not been followed appropriately or if they could argue there would be little "social cost" involved in returning the land. Landowners also had to submit plans for the efficient development of their land if it was returned to them. Under this pretext, 79 percent of the land expropriated under Decree 900 was returned to former landowners, and they and their agents violently reasserted their dominion in rural Guatemala.[48]

Landowners and new agrarian officials also wished to punish peasants who had benefitted from the reform. Citing the need to "modernize agriculture," officials and landowners not only forced almost all the peasants who had received land during the reform off that land, often newly cleared and otherwise improved, but they also instituted more draconian labour regimes on their estates. The result of forcing hundreds of thousands of peasants and family members off their land was a dramatic decline in food production, alleviated only slightly by food aid from the United States. Even with these imports, the Guatemalan university students' newspaper, one of the few sources of independent, critical opinion in the years immediately after the coup, described Guatemalan peasants as a "ghostly army of hunger."[49]

While the post-revolutionary governments forced peasant beneficiaries off land, agrarian officials sought to promote planned agricultural communities of good, market-oriented middle-class farmers, specifically targeted to Ladinos and excluding Mayan peasants who, as "primitive Indians," could not be expected to embrace "modern techniques."[50] Government officials determinedly ignored multiple studies that reiterated the efficiency of peasant agriculture. For example, a USAID study in 1973 pointed out that highland peasants got yields that were more than twenty times per acre what large-scale enterprises received. They invested a surprising amount in their farms and received "significantly higher … value of production" for every dollar invested compared to either large-scale producers in Guatemala or farmers in North America.[51]

Similarly, in a careful and cautiously argued study in the mid-1980s, the geographer Gene Wilken detailed farming techniques among peasants in several areas of highland Guatemala and Mexico. In most locations, peasants farmed very small plots of land, often less than an acre. Wilken described agriculture that was immensely complex, responding to the specific characteristics of soil and climate that changed from field to field. Different products were intercropped in different locations for different effects: to maximize production, to return nitrogen to the soil, to offset acidic or dry or too-damp soils, to provide complete amino acids for diets or to tap markets. Intercropping could involve as many as six plants in a single plot of land. Peasants used a wide range of organic fertilizers, with clear ideas of the different traits of chicken manure compared to that of sheep or goats, most of it determinedly mixed with straw, kitchen scraps and ash to produce the right blend for each field. Wilken argued that peasants were "masters of soil and water management."

Wilken provided a description of the use of vertical space in "dooryard gardens" that was remarkably similar to the glowing accounts of Jamaican *conucos* mentioned in the last chapter: "Plots of no more than 0.1 ha may contain two dozen or more ... plants," each carefully calibrated to take up distinct spaces, from tall trees (mango, papaya) to medium-height trees (banana, peach, citrus) to crops of maize, beans, tomatoes, chile, squash and an understory of herbs, all intertwined with useful vines. No wonder such small-scale peasant agriculture, using intensive labour, produced seemingly miraculous returns. Wilken summarized this by suggesting, "Any lingering images of the lazy, dull, noneconomic peasant farmer must surely have vanished."[52]

Instead of tapping this potential, government officials concentrated their agricultural development efforts on promoting new export crops on the south coast. Chief among these was cotton, which proved to be profitable, briefly. However, beset by pests and falling yields despite intense regimes of chemical pesticide and fertilizers, the land was soon worn out and cotton production on the south coast collapsed, replaced in many areas by sugar. Cotton and sugar producers adopted even more brutal work regimes than the coffee fincas that kept the bells ringing in Chichicastenango during Ruth Bunzel's visit in the 1930s.[53] Every year, poverty forced thousands more Indigenous peasants into these brutal work regimes.[54]

Land hunger and poverty increased, especially in the Indigenous highlands. One notable response from the Guatemalan government and the Institute of Nutrition of Central America and Panama would have seemed comic if not for the deadly circumstance. While pesticide poisoning in the cotton zones skyrocketed, the institute developed a nutritional supplement for infants derived from corn and cotton seed flour, usually considered toxic.

It tried to promote the supplement as the "nutritional miracle of the era" — a poor palliative for the destructive path of increased poverty.[55]

The determination of post-revolutionary governments to paint Mayan peasant agriculture as irredeemably backward, to do whatever they could to promote the interests of large, landed interests, and to prevent any significant redistribution of land ensured the continued poverty of peasants in Guatemala. The 1979 agricultural census revealed that land was even more inequitably distributed than it had been in 1950. Two percent of the farm owners controlled 65 percent of the land. This seriously understates inequality: 55 percent of the population relied on agriculture for a living, but 49 percent of those were landless. Fewer than 500 people, in a population of just under ten million, owned 22 percent of all the land. Land tenure inequality, as a Gini coefficient of inequality, was .85, one of the most inequitable in the world. By the turn of the century, fully 71 percent of the Indigenous population lived in poverty, according to the United Nations.[56]

"The Last Vestiges of Barbarity"

The intense violence of the early 1980s developed its own deeply disturbing internal coherence, driven by multiple impulses. But its genesis was in highland peasant resilience during the 1970s and the continued determination of the government and military to undermine that resilience. After the overthrow of the revolutionary governments in 1954, military officer followed military officer into the presidency. Though they all campaigned vigorously in Guatemala's sham democracy, promising reform, the end of poverty, or in the case of ex-general Miguel Ydígoras Fuentes, a chicken in every pot at least once a week, little changed. Instead of trying to tap their inherent strengths, various regimes actively sought to prevent rural development if it strengthened highland peasant agriculture or assisted peasant organization, apparently frightened that such work might lead to real demands for democracy and change.

In 1976, Guatemala was struck by a horrific earthquake. The worst devastation occurred in Mayan villages in the central highlands. As various sectors in the military government squabbled over access to millions of dollars in aid money, little flowed to the villages. Working with independent aid agencies and the Catholic Church, communities soon took control of the relief and rebuilding efforts, and in the process, spawned a whole generation of community leaders. They soon invigorated community development associations and peasant organizations, most notably peasant co-operatives and the Campesino Unity Committee. Even with the limited resources available to highland peasants, these efforts demonstrated once again the vitality of highland peasant pursuits, and for some in official positions, once again threatened the viability of export agriculture and their visions for Guatemala's future.

Thus, in the late 1970s, before the violence thrust its own demented logic on the country, state-led repression was directed most clearly at expressions of peasant independence. One 1982 Oxfam study found that between 1976 and 1978 in the Department of El Quiché alone, 168 leaders of co-operatives and village organizations were killed; the authors labelled these murders, "the suppression of a rural development movement."[57] The most widely publicized "massacre" of peasants in this early period occurred in 1978 at Panzos, Alta Verapaz, when the military opened fire on mostly Q'eqchi peasants protesting dispossession of their land in the Polochic Valley.[58] In the ensuing years of violence, thousands and thousands of peasants would report, "they flattened our milpa, burned our fields, stole our animals, destroyed our seeds, and prevented us from working in our fields" as the Guatemalan state and elite, a century after Ignacio Solis had urged the elimination of "the last vestiges of barbarity," still sought its elimination.

NOTES

1   Oficina de Derechos Humanos del Arzobispado en Guatemala. *Guatemala: Nunca Más*, Proyecto Interdiocesano de Recuperación de la memoria histórico (Remhi), Tomo 1, 1998..

2   Guatemala, United Nations Mission, *Guatemala: Memory of Silence,* Report of the Commission for the Clarification of History, English language summary, 1999, 20, 23, 17. See also Jim Handy, "The Violence of Dispossession: Guatemala in the Nineteenth and Twentieth Centuries," 281–324, in Sebastian Huhn and Hannes Warnecke-Berger (eds.), *Politics and History of Violence and Crime in Central America,* New York: Palgrave Macmillan, 2017.

3   Guatemala, UN Mission, 17.

4   See George Lovell, "Epidemias y despoblación, 1519–1632," in Jorge Luján Muñoz (ed.), *Historia General de Guatemala* Vol. 2, Guatemala: Fundación para la Cultura y el Desarrollo, 1993, 327–336; George Lovell and Christopher Lutz, *Demography and Empire: A Guide to the Population History of Spanish Central America, 1500–1821,* Boulder: Westview Press, 1995.

5   The classic work on colonial Central America is Murdo McLeod, *Spanish Central America: A Socioeconomic History, 1520–1720,* first published Berkeley: University of California Press, 1973, revised edition Austin: University of Texas Press, 2008; see also William Sherman, *Forced Native Labor in Sixteenth-Century Central America,* Lincoln: University of Nebraska Press, 1979; Robert Carmack, *Historia Social de los Quichés,* Guatemala: José de Pineda Ibarra, 1979. This was not, of course, restricted to Guatemala. Alexander Koch, Chris Brierley, Mark

Maslin, and Simon Lewis argue that the fall in indigenous populations following Spanish conquest led to the removal of more than 100 million hectares of land from agriculture. The resulting reduction in carbon from the atmosphere as land returned to forest might have been a significant cause of the Little Ice Age in Europe that began in the early 1600s. "Earth System Impacts of the European Arrival and Great Dying in the Americas after 1492," *Quaternary Science Reviews,* 207 (2019), 13–36.

6   Stefania Gallina, *Una historia ambiental del café en Guatemala,* Guatemala: AVANCSO, 2009.

7   For a nuanced discussion of the way identities were designated both in official documentation and in local application, see Todd Little-Siebold, "Where Have All the Spaniards Gone: Independent Identities: Ethnicities, Class and the Emergent National State," *Journal of Latin American and Caribbean Anthropology,* 6:2 (2001), 106–133.

8   Matilde González-Izás, *Modernización capitalista, racismo y violencia: Guatemala, 1750–1930,* Mexico: El Colegio de México, 2014. A particularly graphic illustration of this process comes from the Panchoy Valley, where surveyor maps from much of the 19th century show cochineal land in the valley bottom laid out in individually owned plots complete with designated owners, while the hillsides were labeled as undifferentiated "*milperos.*" Through the 19th century, the individually titled valley lands spread out, and after the middle of the century were increasingly marked as coffee fincas. At no time in this century, however, was there an attempt to deal more systematically with the *milpa* land on the hillside. Maps to this effect are available in the Sacatepéquez archives.

9   Rene Reeves, *Ladinos with Ladinos, Indians with Indians: Land, Labor, and Regional Ethnic Conflict in the Making of Guatemala,* Stanford University Press: Stanford, 2006; Arturo Taracena Arriola, *Invención criolla, sueño ladino, pesadilla indígena: Los Altos de Guatemala,* San José: Centro de Investigaciones Regionales de Mesoamérica, 1997; Robert Carmack, *Rebels of Highland Guatemala: The Quiché-Mayas of Momostenango,* Norman: University of Oklahoma Press, 1995. David Carey, "The Heart of the Country: The Primacy of Peasants and Maize in Modern Guatemala," *Journal of Latin American Studies* 51:2 (2019), 273–306.

10 Ralph Lee Woodward Jr., *Rafael Carrera and the Emergence of the Republic of Guatemala, 1821–1871,* Athens: University of Georgia Press, 1993.

11 V. Solórzano, *Evolución económica de Guatemala,* Guatemala City: Seminario de integración social, 1977; M. Rubio Sánchez, "La grana o cochinilla," *Antropología e historia de Guatemala,* 3 (1961), 15–46; G. Bernoulli and J. Kuczynsk cited in J.C. Cambranes, *Aspectos del desarrollo económico y social de Guatemala a la luz de fuentes históricas alemanas, 1868–1885,* Guatemala City: Universidad de San Carlos, 1975, 13, 16, and 21.

12 Carey, "The Heart of the Country," 2019.

13 For a comparison of different patterns of coffee cultivation see Robert Williams, *States and Social Evolution: Coffee and the Rise of National Governments in Central America,* Chapel Hill: University of North Carolina Press, 1994.

14 Reeves, *Ladinos with Ladinos,* 2006; Edgar Esquit, "Identidades politicas indigenas en la época de la privatización de las tierras en Guatemala, finales del

siglo XIX," *Territorios* VIII (Nov. 2013), 75–96.

15 David McCreery, *Rural Guatemala 1760–1940*, Stanford: Stanford University Press, 1994; Vincent Stanzione, *Rituals of Sacrifice: Walking the Face of the Earth on the Sacred Path of the Sun*, Albuquerque: University of New Mexico Press, 2003.

16 George Lovell, "Surviving Conquest: The Maya of Guatemala in Historical Perspective," *Latin American Research Review* 23, 2 (1988), 25–57; Julio Castellanos Cambranes, *Café y campesinos en Guatemala, 1853–1897*, Guatemala: Editorial Universitaria de Guatemala, 1985.

17 First planter cited in *El Democrata* (July 25, 1886) in Guillermo Náñez Falcón, "Erwin Paul Dieseldorff, German Entrepreneur in the Alta Verapaz of Guatemala, 1889–1937," PhD dissertation, Tulane, 1970, 303; second cited in E.C. Higbee, "The Agricultural Regions of Guatemala," *The Geographical Review* 37 (1947), 177–201.

18 David McCreery, "'An Odious Feudalism': *Mandamiento* Labor and Commercial Agriculture in Guatemala, 1858–1920," *Latin American Perspectives* 13: 1 (1986), 99–118; David McCreery, "Debt Servitude in Rural Guatemala, 1876–1936," *Hispanic American Research Review* 63: 4 (1983), 735–739.

19 Jefe Político of Chimaltenango cited in Jorge Mario García LaGuardia, *El pensamiento liberal de Guatemala*, San José, Costa Rica: Educa, 1977, 221.

20 Cited in Carey, "Heart of the Country," 2019, 283.

21 McCreery, "An Odious Feudalism," 1986; Robert Carmack, "Spanish-Indian Relations in Highland Guatemala 1800–1944," in Murdo McLeod and Robert Wasserstrom (eds.), *Spaniards and Indians in Southeastern Mesoamerica*, Lincoln: University of Nebraska Press, 1983, 242–243.

22 R. Burkitt, "Explorations in the Highlands of Western Guatemala," *The Museum Journal of the University of Pennsylvania*, 21 (1930), 58.

23 Cited in Douglas Madigan, "Santiago Atitlán, Guatemala: A Socioeconomic and Demographic History," PhD dissertation, University of Pittsburgh, 1976, 248.

24 J. Steward Lincoln, "An Ethnological Study of Ixile Indians," *Manuscript Collections of Middle American Anthropology (MACA)*, University of Chicago, #1, 1945, 741; Charles Wagley, "Economics of a Guatemalan Village," *American Anthropological Association Memoir* 58 (1941), and Ruth Bunzel's description of debt bondage in Chichicastenango below.

25 Cited in Daniel Wilkinson, *Silence on the Mountain: Stories of Terror, Betrayal, and Forgetting in Guatemala*, Boston: Houghton Mifflin, 2002, 37–38.

26 Ignacio Solis, *Nuestras Artes Industriales 1893*, reprinted in Edgar Barillas, "El problema del Indio durante la Epoca Liberal," 1988, unpublished manuscript.

27 Cited in McCreery, *Rural Guatemala*, 1994, 175.

28 Cited in Carey, "The Heart of the Country," 2019, 300.

29 Chester Lloyd Jones, *Guatemala: Past and Present*, Minneapolis: University of Minnesota Press, 1940, 187–189.

30 Solórzano, *Evolución económica*, 1977; M. Rubio Sánchez, "La grana o cochinilla," 1961, 15–46; G. Bernoulli and J. Kuczynski, cited in Cambranes, *Aspectos del desarrollo*, 1975, 13, 16, and 21.

31 Ruth Leal Bunzel, *Chichicastenango: A Guatemalan Village*, Seattle: University of

Chicago Press, 1959 [1952], 8–9.

32 Bunzel, *Chichicastenango,* 1959, 10.

33 Ibid., 1, 2, 18–23.

34 Ryan Isakson, "No hay ganancia en la milpa: The Agrarian Question, Food Sovereignty, and the On-Farm Conservation of Agrobiodiversity in the Guatemalan Highlands," *Journal of Peasant Studies* 36:4 (2009), 725–759.

35 Bunzel, *Chichicastenango,* 1959, 42–43, 49, 59.

36 Ibid., 30.

37 Robert Redfield, "April Is This Afternoon: Correspondence of Robert Redfield and Sol Tax, 1933–1944," MACA Series LXIII, University of Chicago Library, June 15, 1980, 131–307.

38 Antonio Goubaud Carrera, "Reconnaissance of Northern Guatemala, 1944," *Manuscript Collections of Middle American Anthropology (MACA)* #17, Chicago: University of Chicago Press, 1947.

39 Sol Tax, "The Towns of Lake Atitlán," MACA #13, Chicago: University of Chicago, 1946; Sol Tax, *Penny Capitalism,* Washington: US Government Printing Office, 1953, 11.

40 Government of Guatemala, *Censo agropecuario, 1950,* Guatemala: Dirección general de estadística, vol. 3: 118, vol. 1: 19, 1954.

41 Patrick Chassé, "Produce More to Live Better: Cotton, Corn, and Agrarian Modernization in Guatemala, 1944–1966," PhD dissertation, University of Saskatchewan, 2017, 56.

42 Asamblea Constituyente de 1945. *Diario de sesiones* 464–465.

43 Hector Sierra, "Corn in Guatemala," in I.E. Melhus (ed.), *Plant Research in the Tropics: Research Bulletin 371,* Ames, Iowa: Iowa State College, 1949, 509–512, in Chassé, Produce More to Live Better, 2017, 89–90.

44 Government of Guatemala, *Informe del ciudadano presidente de la república, coronel Jacobo Arbenz Guzmán al congreso,* Guatemala: Secretaria de Propaganda y Divulgación de la Presidencia de la República, 1953, 6.

45 See for example Carlos Manuel Pellecer, "Por la Prosperidad de Nuestra Patria," *Octubre* Oct. 18, 1951, in Chassé, Produce More to Live Better, 2017, 172.

46 See Jim Handy, *Revolution in the Countryside,* Chapel Hill: University of North Carolina Press, 1994, 77–110.

47 Ibid., 137–167.

48 Jim Handy, "Reforma y Contrareforma: La política agraria en Guatemala, 1952–1957," in Julio Castellanos Cambranes (ed.), *500 Años de lucha por la tierra,* Vol. 1, Guatemala City: Facultad Latinoamericana de Ciencias Sociales, 1992, 379–400.

49 "Editorial: Hambre en el Pueblo," *El Estudiante,* July 28, 1955, 1, 4, in Chassé, Produce More to Live Better, 2017, 211.

50 Jorge Arenales, Guatemalan ambassador to the United States, 1956, cited in Chassé, Produce More to Live Better, 2017, 216.

51 USAID, *Small Farm Policy Analysis,* Washington, 1975, 8, 28; M. Gollas-Quintero, "History and Economic Theory in the Analysis of the Development of Guatemalan Indian Agriculture," PhD dissertation, University of Wisconsin, 1969, 170–171.

52 Wilken, *Good Farmers,* 1987, esp. 41, 49, 249, 250, 263.

53 Elizabeth Oglesby, "Politics at Work: Elites, Labor and Agrarian Modernization in Guatemala, 1980–2000," PhD dissertation, University of California, Berkeley, 2002.

54 Jim Handy, *Gift of the Devil*, Toronto: Between the Lines, 1984, 205–222.

55 "Un Producto Nacional Que Puede Ser Motivo de Una Gran Industria," *Impacto*, May 28, 1959, in Chassé, Produce More to Live Better, 2017, 240.

56 Government of Guatemala, *III Censo Nacional Agropecuario*, 1979; Government of Guatemala, *IV Censo Nacional Agropecuario*, 2004; United Nations Development Program, *Guatemala: una agenda para el desarrollo humano*, 2003; United Nations Development Program, *Informe nacional de desarrollo humano*, 2005.

57 Sheldon Davis and Julie Hodson, *Witnesses to Political Violence in Guatemala: The Suppression of a Rural Development Movement*, Oxfam America Impact Audit, 1982, 15; among numerous works that focus on attacks on peasant livelihoods during this period, see also Beatrice Manz, *Paradise in Ashes: A Guatemalan Journey of Courage, Terror, and Hope, Vol. 8*, Berkeley: University of California Press, 2004.

58 For the fullest discussion of the massacre, see Greg Grandin, *The Last Colonial Massacre: Latin America in the Cold War*, Chicago: University of Chicago Press, 2004.

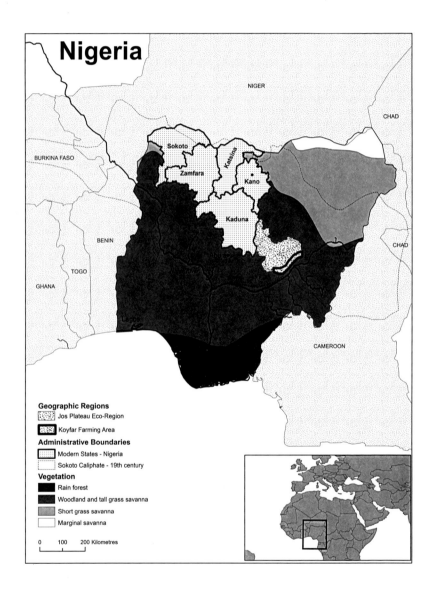

Nigeria

NIGER

CHAD

BURKINA FASO

Sokoto

Zamfara

Katsina

Kano

Kaduna

BENIN

TOGO

GHANA

Lagos

CHAD

CAMEROON

Geographic Regions
- Jos Plateau Eco-Region
- Koyfar Farming Area

Administrative Boundaries
- Modern States - Nigeria
- Sokoto Caliphate - 19th century

Vegetation
- Rain forest
- Woodland and tall grass savanna
- Short grass savanna
- Marginal savanna

0   100   200 Kilometres

5 Nigerian Smallholders: Masters of the Environment

Guatemalan Mayan campesinos were caught in the grip of a particularly rapacious form of agrarian capitalism, one seeking to ensure Mayan rural dwellers would provide the labour that coffee, cotton and sugar growers needed, at prices they wanted to pay. Its virulence was fuelled partly by racism and partly by fear that any relaxing of repression would lead back to the dangerous reforms of the Arbenz administration.

Peasants in most of West Africa have been under similar assault: a combination of shifting policies that over the years helped impoverish peasant agriculture. Despite limited population levels in most of West Africa historically, the spectre of Malthus was constantly invoked to justify attacks on peasant livelihoods. Colonizers sought to tame, control and tax peasants. Newly independent governments in the second half of the 20th century tried to build national economies on the backs of peasant labourers. Development agencies and advisors, beholden to whatever trend caught their fancy, devised schemes to alter national economies, almost all involving the transfer of surplus from peasant production. Ignoring its devastating consequences elsewhere, those proffering green revolution solutions attempted to apply technological fixes to practices that were not broken, and in the process they assiduously worked to undermine the underlying strengths of peasant agriculture in West Africa.

Malthus's ghost continued to hover over West African peasants, as did the many erroneous ideas about the West African environment. Colonial officials and development practitioners saw either an aggressive and too exuberant nature that needed discipline to tame, or a nature too easily degraded by too many people. They saw deforestation where none existed. They imagined violent environments with populations doomed to fight over scarce natural resources, rather than people struggling in the face of indifferent or worse policy, and fighting, often, over too-abundant resources. All these faulty visions led to attacks on peasants in the name of the state, development or the environment. This was a remarkably consistent campaign given that through it all, what worked in West Africa most often was peasant smallholder agriculture.

This chapter explores that history, focusing specifically on Nigeria from the immediate post-independence period to the turn of the century. It outlines how the promised prosperity following independence failed to materialize, partly due to deeply ingrained prejudices in centuries of writing about West African peasant livelihoods. This chapter contrasts these affronts by examining the advantages of widespread, complex and sophisticated polyculture cropping systems and the very real, hard-won abundance that West African, particularly Nigerian, peasants have been able to wring from an often fragile land and a society under threat.

"A Vast, Uncivilised and Unfed Population"

One of the most persistent myths about West Africa is that it has been perpetually over-populated. This myth has been tied to two preoccupations: justifying the transatlantic slave trade and misconceptions about the relationship between population levels and supposed environmental degradation.

Those who defended the slave trade against critiques of the "evil trade … buying and selling peaceable free men, as one buys and sells animals" — that began almost immediately after the first large shipment of slaves from Africa to Portugal in 1444 — often countered that there were too many people living in barbaric fashion in West Africa. Capuchin monks in the middle of the 16th century, for example, depicted West Africa as resembling a "continuous and black anthill," so dense was the population. In such circumstances, being transported across the Atlantic "saved them from Guinea's fire and tyranny and barbarism and brutality, where without law or God, they live like savage beasts." Such arguments continued until the end of the slave trade.[1]

These self-serving misconceptions of West Africa endured well past the end of the transatlantic slave trade. For example, the *Economist* newspaper, attempting to justify its support for a southern victory in the civil war while still brandishing its anti-slavery credentials, argued that "Africa had a vast, uncivilised, and unfed population" and that since the European encounter with Africa the proper role for West Africans had been to provide labour elsewhere. The transport of millions of men, women and children from West Africa that occurred during the slave trade was to be seen as neither a calamity nor a crime. Rather, it was "a curious fact in the natural history of man" that needed neither apology nor much careful consideration.[2] Explanations that minimized the brutality of the transatlantic slave trade through references to West Africa's supposedly over-abundant population continued well into the 20th century.

One expression of colonial arrogance was Europeans' presumption that they understood the African environment. By the end of the 19th century, many Europeans were convinced that they — and only they — understood scientific and natural laws. They saw themselves as living outside of nature and no longer buffeted by the changing fortunes of a fickle climate or dependent on natural processes for agriculture, which they viewed as an important measure of progress and development. This arrogance was perhaps most harmful in Europeans' beliefs that they understood environmental processes in the Sahel and Savanna regions of West Africa. European colonists saw there a mostly dry region of scrubland broken by a few thickets of trees. They saw a substantial population engaged in pastoral and agricultural subsistence and believed there was a direct relationship between a presumed "deforestation" and the activities of these cultivators.

European naturalists, geographers and colonial officials developed an environmental history and agricultural policies based on that history. They also developed an industry of environmental specialists working for governments and development agencies who depended on that history. They attempted to limit peasant and semi-nomadic pastoral activities as a measure both to control populations and to stop this supposed degradation. This portrayal of the Sahel as an environment degraded by too many people pursuing inappropriate livelihoods is now widely seen as erroneous. Nonetheless, the narrative had a surprisingly tenacious existence, repeated time and again by well-meaning policymakers until the end of the 20th century.

Much of this derives from what James McCann has called the "degradation narrative": the argument that the African environment was once in a kind of stasis or balance, which was subsequently degraded by too many people. This argument was employed to great effect by colonial regimes seeking to legitimize colonial exploits. The French, for example, justified their rule in Morocco and Algeria by arguing that they would return an area degraded and deforested by pastoralists to the "fertile plains" that once provided Rome with wheat. They ignored the fact that the region was already exporting more wheat than it had during the Roman era. Nonetheless, reforesting this region and curtailing the activity of peasants and pastoralists, colonial officials asserted, would turn Algeria into the granary of France.[3]

Elsewhere, in humid forested regions of West Africa, colonists were equally confused about environmental processes. Europeans were almost always uncomfortable in the tropics — often for good reason as they remained susceptible to tropical maladies even after the widespread use of quinine (derived from cinchona trees smuggled out of the Peruvian Andes). But this discomfort went beyond such practical considerations. As one British doctor in West Africa said of the European living in the tropics in the early 20th century:

> From early morn till dewey eve he is in a state of unrest — ants at breakfast, flies at lunch, and termites at dinner, with a new species of moth every evening in his coffee.... There is no escape, and the unceasing attentions of the voracious insect world, he is driven to bed by his lamp being extinguished by the hordes which fly by night, only to be kept at wake by the reiterated cry of the brain fever bird or the local chorus of frogs. Never at rest, Always an on-guardedness.[4]

In such regions, colonial officials saw limitless fertility and potential abundance that only needed to be controlled, tapped by labour, disciplined and directed appropriately by European authorities. When this luxurious growth proved not to adapt well to export crops, colonial opinion turned full circle and dismissed the region as inherently and irrevocably infertile. In both instances, misguided opinion often led to disastrous policies.

Mistaken views of the African environment and the supposedly deleterious effects of too many people and too many peasants worsened, if anything, after independence. This was especially the case in the late 1960s and early 1970s, as various publications, importantly and appropriately, warned about the environmental consequences of contemporary capitalism's fascination with growth and cavalier attitude to various types of environmental pollution. Soon though, these arguments were hijacked by those warning about population growth, especially among peasants in materially poor countries. These publications predicted both unchecked population growth and coming famine. Such predictions grew increasingly alarming in the mid-1970s in the face of years of drought in northern Nigeria and other areas of West Africa. In all instances, peasants and small-scale farmers and pastoralists were represented as the worst culprits in the supposed forthcoming environmental and demographic catastrophe.

The hold these misconceptions had on those writing about economic development and the environment in Africa helps explain the impact of a remarkably ill-informed argument by Garret Hardin in 1968. A professor of Human Ecology at the University of California at Santa Barbara, Hardin published a short article entitled "The Tragedy of the Commons." In this, he attempted to argue that all access to common property leads to over-population, over-exploitation of resources and environmental and human disaster. Hardin provided no evidence from any real commons, nor any understanding of the complex mechanisms that existed in hundreds of thousands of commons around the world. Yet his hypothetical example, set clearly in an imagined Africa in which "the inherent logic of the commons remorselessly generates tragedy," was all that many people needed to "prove" that such a logic existed.[5]

Neo-Malthusian arguments linking population increase, environmental degradation and poverty continued in the years following Hardin's work: *The Population Bomb* by Paul and Anne Ehrlich, published the same year as Hardin's article, was followed by the more thoughtful *Limits to Growth* in 1972, and another article by Hardin, even more erroneous and misconceived than his original "Tragedy of the Commons," in 1974.[6] The common thread in these works was the perception — sometimes buried, often explicit — that increased poverty and environmental degradation were — as Malthus warned two centuries earlier — the result of allowing peasants to continue to reproduce without suffering fully the consequences of their irrational attachment to the land.

Similar arguments re-emerged in the years preceding the bicentenary of Malthus's original publication of *An Essay on the Principle of Population* in 1798. One of the most notorious examples of this trend was presented in an apocalyptic vision by Robert Kaplan, in an article for the *Atlantic* entitled "The Coming Anarchy: How Scarcity, Crime, Overpopulation and Disease Are Rapidly Destroying the Social Fabric of our Planet" in 1994.[7] The article formed the basis for two of Kaplan's later books. As the title suggests, his work promised a future of increased poverty, rampant violence, disease, human degradation and conflict caused primarily by overpopulation, en-vironmental collapse and resource depletion. He based much of his work on West Africa. Kaplan's article drew from the somewhat more academic work often associated with Tad Homer-Dixon, then at the University of Toronto. Homer-Dixon led a team called the Environmental Change and Acute Conflict Project, its work summarized in Homer-Dixon's 1999 book, *Environment, Scarcity and Violence.* The major argument in the book was that scarcity of renewable resources — what he called environmental scarcity — can contribute to civil violence, insurgencies and ethnic clashes, and that due to population growth in the coming decades, the incidence of such violence will increase. Like Kaplan, Homer-Dixon pointed to West Africa as one of the prime sites for such "environmental violence."[8]

There have been some convincing criticisms of these works. Indeed, the major wars in the heart of the region discussed by both Kaplan and Homer-Dixon were not fought over scarce resources. Rather, they were driven primarily by attempts to control singularly valuable and at times abundant resources: illegally logged wood, and in the most famous case, forest diamonds. That such conflicts took place in the context of significant poverty and that they contributed to increased poverty are not in question, of course, but cause and effect most certainly are.

How do we explain these continued myths about the African environment and its supposed enemies? One part of that explanation comes from what people — colonial officials and later development experts — expected to see in Africa. Roderick Neumann describes how on a visit to a wilderness park in Tanzania, one of the accompanying British ecologists proclaimed at the sight of savanna, a green river and no obvious signs of human inhabitants, "This is the way Africa should look."[9] With such ingrained expectations, all human disruption of the environment was perceived as degradation. It was easy, therefore, to perceive examples of human-induced environmental change as evidence of overpopulation.

As Ester Boserup pointed out many decades ago, many of the applications of Malthusian ideas to arguments about population levels in Africa failed to understand the flexibility and adaptability of smallholder agriculture. Boserup argued that contrary to the views of Malthus, increased population levels most often led to more intensive and effective use of land through the application of more labour on each acre. This often involved a transition to less shifting cultivation, more permanent fields and careful efforts to maintain soil fertility and moisture levels. Though some see Boserup's work as suffering from her own preconceived ideas about a natural "progression" from shifting to permanent cultivation, her general arguments about the adaptability of smallholder agriculture and its ability to change in the face of increased populations have been reinforced by subsequent authors.[10] Numerous other works have pointed out the complex relationships between population levels, peasant agriculture and the environment in West Africa. Most have reiterated Boserup's findings that most of West Africa remains sparsely populated and that it is a region where agriculturalists have readily and efficiently adapted to localized increases in population levels. Nonetheless, a too-ready tendency to blame environmental and nutritional challenges on the perceived failings of peasants has permeated policy in and writing about West Africa for more than a century. In the process, the very real strengths of West African peasant agriculture have been effaced.

Imagining Unlimited Supplies of Labour

In the 1860s, the *Economist*, while excusing slavery, also predicted the brutal colonial regimes in West Africa that followed the end of the slave trade. Worried constantly about the precarious supply of cotton from the US south and doubtful about India's ability to provide the necessary replacement, the paper argued that West Africa held the most promise as the saviour of the English textile industry: a prelude to the scramble for Africa with cotton as one of its driving forces. Yet for West Africa to play its appropriate role in providing raw material for British industrialization, labour needed to be organized and peasants forced to provide that labour. Given what we know now about the abuses of obligatory cultivation and labour regimes associated with cotton cultivation in Africa, the paper's prediction about next steps is remarkably chilling. In 1861 it argued:

> The one necessary essential to the development of these new sources of prosperity is the arrangement of some industrial system under which very large bodies of dark labourers will work willingly under a very few European supervisors. It is not individual labour which is required, but organised labour, labour so scientifically arranged that the maximum result shall be obtained at a minimum cost … it is clear that the dark races must in some way or other be induced to obey white men willingly.[11]

Colonial regimes, establishing themselves in West Africa in the late 19th century, were driven by many of these concerns. In the last quarter of the 19th century, a menagerie of European powers carved up Africa in what Crawford Young has called "a collective intoxication of colonial expansionism." By the end of the century, only Ethiopia remained outside of formal colonial control. This process occurred as other European powers, somewhat desperately, sought to emulate British industrialization and gain resources (primarily cotton) and markets to assist in that goal. Young argues that this scramble occurred, not coincidentally, "with the historical zenith of virulent racism … the arrogance of race was never stronger than at the moment of colonial onslaught on Africa."[12] These obsessions played a role in determining colonial regimes' relationships to peasants.

Intent on reorganizing labour into some agrarian resemblance of an industrial system and inspired by the same disdain for the "clumsy" labour of smallholders exhibited by the modern "improvers" in Europe, colonial regimes in West African were obsessed with forcing labour, products and taxes from African peasants. In many parts of Africa, rapacious regimes of coerced or forced cultivation destroyed indigenous agricultural systems and decimated population levels. In West Africa generally, and in colonial Nigeria particularly, colonial policy was less brutally enforced and its results more diffuse than the coerced rubber collection or cotton cultivation schemes found elsewhere in Africa. This occurred partly because the British in the Protectorate of the Northern Province (what became Nigeria after independence) established in 1903 lacked the administrative apparatus necessary for such blatant coercion. It was also because, to a certain extent, West African agriculturalists proved to be relatively adept at producing the colonial products Britain needed, fairly quickly providing groundnuts, cotton and cacao for export. Nonetheless, colonial policies both impoverished smallholder agriculture and set the stage for the inappropriate governmental and development policy that followed. To understand these effects, we need to trace colonial ideas about agriculture in Nigeria.

Northern Nigeria at the time of the Protectorate's establishment was encompassed by the remarkable Sokoto Caliphate. At the turn of the century, this area of dryland savanna, which included the emirates in what became northern Nigeria, supported about ten million people. Most were dependent on a complex array of agricultural systems, including a mix of swidden agriculture and permanent fields, especially in better-watered riverine environments or close to population centres. A well-established peasantry paid taxes to the caliphate state, but there was also extensive slavery, mostly in the production of groundnuts for export.[13] Peasant agriculture relied on intercropped millet, sorghum and cowpeas, the advantages of which are discussed further below. But as Michael Watts points out, there was an infinite variety of alterations to this combination depending on circumstance. Better-watered riverine locations also produced manioc, sugar, onions, tomatoes, rice, tobacco, cotton, henna and much else. Areas close to large population centres were intensively farmed and might have supported population levels of 300 people per square mile. Elsewhere, swidden agriculture was followed, the whole region appearing, in the words of Michael Watts, as "farmed parklands" maintaining a host of useful trees and shrubs.[14]

The colonial regime initially reinforced the power of the Muslim emirs over land and labour, at the same time working to end slavery in the region. But the peasantry was considered the bedrock of the colonial state, meant to pay high levels of rigorously imposed taxes to cover the state's costs and to supply Britain with the products necessary for continued industrialization. Taxes imposed on peasant producers played multiple roles. They paid the cost of empire, forced peasants to produce goods for the market and especially for the colonial trading companies, reinforced the authority of the colonial regime and its agents, and — as colonial officials constantly reiterated — served to accustom African peasants to labour, to "civilize" themselves through work."[15]

In Nigeria, peasants had been used to paying taxes to the Sokoto Caliphate, but this system had been flexible and varied according to the harvest and to peasant needs. As Watts says, "In sharp contrast to the pre-colonial Caliphal revenue system, colonial taxes were regular, predictable, and above all rigid."[16] Taxes helped propel peasants to produce groundnuts, cotton and cacao for British merchants. While some of these crops, such as groundnuts, could be grown in intercropped agriculture systems, and others, like cacao, were often grown in regions recently made accessible to peasants, still others — particularly cotton — competed with food production lands. All drew labour from food production, while siphoning the surplus from peasant production through heavy taxation. Watts argues that all of this helped lead the peasantry to the edge of food insecurity. Colonial officials blamed scarcity and famine on an "improvident peasantry, a population of congenital reprobates."[17]

On the ground, colonial policy towards the peasantry shifted continually. Pressures to coerce the peasantry into the production of export crops resulted in famine. By the 1920s, with disappointing results in cotton, the most anticipated colonial product, the colonial government in Nigeria turned its focus to "improving" peasant agriculture. The results were predictably unfortunate. These experiments stopped briefly in the 1930s, when a coterie of colonial officials became impressed by the "active innovation and invention" that occurred in peasant agriculture. As Howard Jones, an employee in the Nigerian Department of Agriculture, pointed out in a publication in 1936, one needed to spend some time in the field to understand the benefits of smallholder agricultural processes:

> The plants are not growing at random, but have been planted at proper distances on hillocks of soil arranged in such a way that when rain falls it does not waterlog the plants, nor does it pour off the surface and wash away the fine soil: the stumps of bushes and trees are left for the yams to climb upon and the oil palms are left standing because they yield valuable fruits; and although several kinds of plants are growing together, they were not sown at the same time nor will they be reaped together: they are rather

successive crops planted in such a way that the soil is always occupied and is neither dried up by the sun nor leached out by the
rain, as it would be if it were left bare at any time.[18]

This period of grudging appreciation for peasant agriculture soon passed.
During and after the Second World War, Britain sought to rebuild itself
partly on the backs of its colonies, especially the backs of peasants in Africa.
It demanded more products and increased income from them. Partly this
was provided by colonial marketing schemes that obliged cacao, groundnut
and cotton producers to market their crops through monopolies. Products
were purchased far below the world price, with the colonial government
pocketing the difference. The Groundnut and Cotton Marketing Boards
established in colonial Nigeria in 1947, for example, had accumulated a
surplus of £81 million by 1954. In addition, the colonial regimes once again
sought to reorganize agriculture through usually disastrous and always
expensive mechanization schemes. The colonial government's Mechanical
Cultivation Scheme for rice in Sierra Leone, for example, never produced
more than 4 percent of the rice grown, yet took 80 percent of the colonial
government's agricultural budget.[19] And in Nigeria in 1947, the colonial
government's first ten-year plan for agriculture also focused on transforming
peasant agriculture through mechanization. In one scheme, given twenty-
four-acre plots of land, farmers were estimated to have to perform 408
weeks of labour in one six-week period. These all proved to be "unmitigated
disasters" according to Michael Watts.[20]

As Kavita Philip has commented in the context of India, post-colonial
subjects did not easily shed the identities assigned to them by the colonizer.[21]
This is no doubt also true of post-colonial governments. Independent
regimes in West Africa, as in other parts of the continent, rejected many
of the constraints placed on them by their former colonial masters. Yet
almost all of them continued with policies meant to control, tax, and in
many ways impoverish, while ostensibly improving the lives of, peasants.
Most continued with monopolistic marketing boards that underpaid for
peasant products. Many also continued mechanization schemes, promoting
industrial-type agriculture at the expense of peasants. In Ghana, for example,
large-scale mechanized rice cultivation in the 1970s depended on mostly
hidden subsidies of up to 85 percent of the cost of production to allow it
to compete with small-scale production of foodstuffs.[22]

In these schemes, independent governments were advised by development agencies and experts. One need not refer to such ill-intentioned
though influential works as W.W. Rostow's *Stages in Economic Growth*, with

his praise of the modernizing effects of colonialism and his disdain for tradition, to find evidence of this continued prejudice against peasant production. Supposedly informed comments from more thoughtful advisors and academics through the 1990s sang the same song about the need to change peasant livelihoods, chain peasants more securely to the state and use their labour for alternative visions of economic development.

Goran Hyden, writing primarily about Tanzania, lamented a peasantry "uncaptured" by the state and argued that peasant independence was the "principal structural constraint to development." Regimes throughout Africa, he argued, needed to find better ways to exploit and "subordinate the peasants to the demands of state policies."[23] Similarly, Keith Hart, a well-known development advisor for the World Bank and USAID in the 1970s and 1980s, argued that the major problem facing West African economies was the prevalence of a peasantry, insufficiently coerced into producing a surplus for the market. He counselled ways to make the state's involvement in agricultural production both indispensable and lucrative, primarily through large-scale infrastructure expenditures such as dams or the continued use of marketing boards controlled by the state. As he expressed it, "Agricultural intensification means getting people to work harder, and that undertaking requires coercion."[24]

Even thoughtful and well-meaning advisors counselled measures that attacked peasant livelihoods in ways little different from colonial regimes. W.A. Lewis was one of them. Born in Santa Lucia, he was an advisor to Kwame Nkrumah following Ghanaian independence, the first director of the United Nations Special Fund (the precursor to the United Nations Development Program) and the co-recipient of the Nobel Prize in Economics in 1979. He wrote numerous books and articles, but his most influential work was a short article entitled "Economic Development with Unlimited Supplies of Labour" in 1954. It was to this "model" that the Nobel committee referred when announcing the award. Lewis's argument there and elsewhere was complex, but it was clearly drawn from his background in British economic history, which he studied for his PhD at the London School of Economics. Rural West Africa, he argued, was marked by "a few highly capitalized plantations, surrounded by a sea of peasants." The marginal productivity of labour in this sea of peasants approached zero — that is, labour could be taken from peasant agriculture with no penalty in lost food production. These peasants needed to supply unlimited labour to a modern, capitalized industrial sector. As agriculture also needed to supply the capital for investment in industry, he cautioned against allowing peasants to reap any rewards from an increase in agricultural productivity. Most importantly, urban food prices needed to be kept low — through various measures designed to reduce peasant incomes — to help control any increase in industrial wages.[25] It was partly Lewis's influence that prompted Nkrumah to attempt to tap the surplus of peasant producers and of small-scale cocoa farmers to subsidize both failed industries and unsuccessful large-scale agricultural enterprises. Lewis's influence was felt through much of West Africa and similar policies — *mutatis mutandis* — were followed to equally disastrous effect in most of the region.

The Green Revolution: "The Chemical Genetic System"

In the 1970s and increasingly into the 1980s and beyond, government policies began again to understand the benefits of small-scale production. The multiple failures of African agriculture in the years immediately following independence — even in those countries like Nigeria that still had reasonably productive, diverse agricultural sectors at independence — and heightened levels of urban unemployment led policymakers to focus not on how labour could be drawn from agriculture (as Lewis counselled) but on how agriculture could efficiently employ more labour.[26] Unfortunately, much of this became entangled with new schemes for improving peasant agriculture linked to the green revolution. (A fuller discussion of the genesis of green revolution technology and its promotion, particularly in Asia, is provided in the next chapter, on Kerala.)

Emboldened by what was at first perceived to be the success of new hybrid varieties of rice and wheat in India that required increased water and chemical fertilizers but promised increased yields, research and promotion of similar new varieties were pushed for Africa. Much of this research was funded by the United Nations and the Consultative Group on International Agricultural Research and focused on the International Institute of Tropical Agriculture in Ibadan, Nigeria. Familiar tropes were trotted out to justify these new crops — which one critic referred to as the "Chemical Genetic System." He suggested that proponents of the system deliberately ignored any complaints from smallholders in Africa, and that such approaches fit poorly with existing agriculture, and indeed, with existing climate and geographies in Africa. As he said, "The ethos of the Green Revolution was [that] the CG System stood between runaway population increase and widespread starvation, and that beggars ought not to be choosers."[27]

Green revolution technology and crops were singularly unsuccessful in much of Africa in the late 20th century. Even in Nigeria, where the Institute of Tropical Agriculture centre was located, agricultural output continued to fall, and Nigeria, like much of West Africa, needed to import food.

Nonetheless, in 2006 the Bill and Melinda Gates Foundation provided the funds to jumpstart the new Alliance for a Green Revolution program designed to modernize African agriculture. The arguments by those pushing most insistently for a new green revolution in Africa seem at first glance convincing. The usual premise is perfectly logical: African governments and developmental agencies neglected agriculture through the latter part of the 20th century, and this neglect precipitated falling agricultural production and dependence on imported food or food aid.[28]

Arguments in favour of the new green revolution in Africa invariably pointed to rapidly increasing yields of grains in parts of India as evidence of what it might achieve. They ignored the already well-understood negative impacts of the green revolution in India, felt in falling farmer incomes, widespread environmental problems and reduced access to food. (One of the many statistical examples that illustrate this shows that between the early 1970s and the 1990s, the percentage of the Indian population with access to less than 2,400 calories a day increased from 56 to 75 percent). One needs to ask how such evidence could so easily be ignored by those advocating for a new green revolution in Africa.[29]

If anything, the arguments for a revived green revolution in Africa are even more misplaced than they turned out to be in India. These proposals almost invariably dismissed one of the great strengths of smallholder agriculture in Africa, particularly in West Africa: the widespread practice of polycropping. One example is the widely read article that Xinshen Diao, Derek Headey and Michael Johnson published in the journal *Agricultural Economics* in 2008. The authors start off explaining how recent increases in food prices might be the spur necessary to prompt significant new attention on food production in Africa — in the form of a new green revolution. They argue that the intent is to find a way to reduce food insecurity and thereby increase economic well-being in Africa. But the article turns out to have little to do with how the poor — rural or urban — might get more access to food. Instead, it focuses almost exclusively on the economic growth benefits of concentrating on a few key staple products for domestic production and export. Despite suggestions that this might "serve as an engine for income growth for a majority of smallholder African farmers" there is no appreciation evidenced here for the complexity of smallholder farming in Africa.[30] Indeed, the article focuses instead on altering livestock production to rely on feed provided by grains currently used for human consumption. It is difficult to envision how doubling the use of grains and root crops to feed animals instead of humans might lead to increased food security, even in a world inhabited by agricultural economists. There is certainly no appreciation shown for the efficiencies demonstrated by intercropped homestead land in the Kofyar hills described at length below.

In one other particularly noteworthy article in *The African Technology and Development Forum* in 2011, William Kerr, an agricultural economist at the University of Saskatchewan, Canada's largest agricultural college, suggested that both Malthus and somehow — despite all logic — the Irish potato famine proved the importance of free markets in promoting innovation and increased food security.[31] Again, there is no sense of understanding in these publications of the logic behind polycropping, nor of the damage that would be done to such agricultural systems with the employment of hybrid seeds requiring intensive chemical and other inputs. With such disregard for history, actual agricultural practice, and indeed, logic, it is not difficult to see how a new green revolution for Africa could be proposed as a solution to policies that have for too long attacked peasant livelihoods and production.

"In the Wake of the Affluent Society"

In a work originally published in French in 1991, the French economist Serge Latouche provided cogent arguments against many of the assumptions then in development literature and practice, especially in West Africa. One of Latouche's arguments was that those who constantly referred to the "failures" of West Africa were looking for the wrong things. Viewed from a different framework — evaluating West Africans' success in providing themselves with the important things in life — he argued the region, and West African peasants in particular, enjoyed some surprising successes and strengths. To understand these strengths, he suggested, one had to go beyond the gleaming palaces of a borrowed modernity in the capital cities and past the slums of the cities that so frightened Robert Kaplan and look to peasant Africa. There, he suggested, one would find an African society that functions.[32] We should follow Latouche there now.

We have only recently begun to trace how deeply African society and agriculture were affected by centuries of the slave trade. Predatory states, whether those providing slaves for the transatlantic slave trade or Muslim regimes finding victims for the Saharan trade — or for their own production of groundnuts for export, as in the Sokoto Caliphate — made life especially precarious. Numerous groups were forced to abandon fertile and favoured areas for more isolated, more easily defended locales. Others needed to shift from crops that left agriculturalists open to attack in favour of less nutritionally dense or diverse ones that could be cultivated closer to home or were harder for marauding bands to identify. In many cases in West Africa, this meant shifting from an agriculture based around sorghum or millet to one dependent on manioc.[33] Despite these afflictions, A. G. Hopkins argues that on the whole the agricultural history of pre-colonial West Africa "is a story of innovation rather than stagnation."[34]

One of the great strengths of this story of innovation is the importance and efficacy of polycropping. More than 80 percent of the agricultural land in West Africa is polycropped.[35] Supported and promoted wisely, it offers a range of important benefits that should have provided — and could still provide — the basis for efficient agriculture in West Africa. As the description by Howard Jones from 1936 cited above suggests, many of those who bothered to look carefully at polycropping among West African smallholders have been singularly impressed with the results. Successful polycropping uses land, labour, and even more essentially in many locales, water to its greatest possible benefit. A polycropped field adapted through careful experimentation and knowledge of the local environment and conditions produces significantly more on each acre of land. Even though these systems are labour-intensive, a polycropped field uses labour more efficiently than a monocropped field.[36] Different plants in a successful polycropped field occupy varied spaces in the field, not only on the ground itself but in the air as crops vary in height. Perhaps even more importantly, they have different spatial requirements under the ground as roots establish themselves at different depths in the soil. In Nigeria, for example, cowpeas and groundnuts have deeper root systems than cereals and thus compete less for nutrients. As each crop germinates and develops at its own rhythm, combined they use soil moisture levels more efficiently.

Another important advantage of such polycropping is the way it spreads labour demands more evenly. Many decades ago, Ester Boserup pointed out that in Africa, one of the bottlenecks for increased agricultural intensity was the amount of labour needed to harvest or work crops at peak times. That is, even though significant surplus labour might be available through much of the year, new crops could not be added if they, too, contributed to labour demands during peak times.[37] Such variable labour requirements have meant that peasants have often been small handicraft producers, occupying what would otherwise be idle hours with productive work, even if the hourly rewards on such labour have not been high — a commonality with English wool weavers, Indian cotton spinners and Guatemalan handicraft producers. African smallholders, too, occupy some of their time with handicraft production. However, an even more important way to spread labour demand is through polycropping. As Paul Richards noted, such agriculture helps "flatten out the labour input profile."[38] And as Matt Liebman suggested in his

survey of polyculture cropping systems around the world, its prevalence in
so many places worldwide suggests the many benefits such systems offer.[39]

Successful polyculture cropping requires familiarity with an environment and its constraints along with a willingness to experiment. Done well,
such systems can even turn some less than favourable environments into
extremely productive ones. One interesting example of such adaptation to
adversity is the Kofyar in eastern Nigeria.[40]

The Kofyar are a linguistically aligned group of people who farm on the
southeastern flanks of the Jos Plateau, in a region described as sub-humid
savanna. These "hill farmers," as Robert Netting calls them, settled on the
rugged slopes of the plateau as a refuge from Muslin slave raiders and later
European troops. The first official European contact came in 1909; the first
British act was to conduct a census as a prelude to imposing taxes. Relations
between the British and the Kofyar remained tense for decades to follow.
In the 1930s, after one assistant district officer was killed over taxes, the
British destroyed ten hill villages and forced about 10 percent of the Kofyar
population from their homes. These refugees were not allowed to return
until the end of that decade. It took until the second half of the 20th century
for the Kofyar to feel secure enough to expand agricultural pursuits to more
favourable agricultural land at the base of the plateau.

The Kofyar were thus forced into a rugged, constrained environment.
Both colonial and developmentalist discourse should have prepared us to
find that the Kofyar suffered from all the expected disorders of marginal-
ized, traditional and decidedly unmodern agriculturalists on a constrained
and somewhat inhospitable land base. Instead, we find that they developed
an intensive agricultural system that adapted remarkably to the peculiar
constraints of their environment. Kofyar agriculture revolves around the
homestead fields (*mar koepang*). These fields are small — a Kofyar family
of five might have about 2.5 acres of land including homestead fields and
some bush farms — but intensively farmed and carefully maintained despite
the challenging hill environment. The fields are extensively terraced and are
worked in a variety of intricate ways to prevent runoff, maintain soil moisture
and prevent standing water from harming crops. The terraces provide a series
of relatively flat benches on the hillside that are suitable for farming, but
each terrace is also worked into a series of furrows or ridges usually set in a
square pattern. Crops are planted on the tops of the furrows to keep them
out of standing water, while the square's ridges prevent runoff and maintain
water. But like the Central American *milpa* farmers Wilkens described as
masters of hydrology, the Kofyar employ different techniques on different
types of fields at varying degrees of slope. On flatter fields, they employ a

series of broken ridges and furrows that capture and direct the water, allowing it to flow slowly downhill while directing it to where it is most needed.

Kofyar nutrition is based primarily around a kind of porridge made from sorghum and millet. Like the three sisters of a Mayan *milpa* — corn, frijole and squash — Kofyar agriculture is most often centred around the combination of sorghum, millet and cowpeas grown together. They also grow a remarkable variety of crops attuned to specific localized conditions. Acha or hungry rice, for example, can be grown in places too wet to support other crops. It can also be sown early and harvested in time to allow a crop of millet on the same ground in a single year. Pumpkin and cucurbits are likewise sown early, before the soil is wet enough to sustain millet and sorghum. Groundnuts are alternated with acha as a means of replenishing nitrogen in the soil. Along with these, Kofyar grow coco yams, sweet potatoes, cassava, okra, maize and string beans. Most often these are intercropped and grown so thickly as to naturally prevent weeds. There is virtually no natural forest either on the hills or in the plains at the base of the hills, but there are plenty of trees as part of either the household or the bush gardens. These include oil and fan palms, camarium, locust bean, papaya, mango and fig trees. Most households also have a few cotton bushes from which to spin their own textiles.

While all the Kofyar use many of the same crops throughout their home fields, the mix differs depending on local conditions, soil quality and needs. The Kofyar use a complex system for classifying soil and recognize that different crops do better in certain types of soils. Some areas are also subject to prevailing winds that can damage sorghum, so planting is reserved for those parts of their fields that are less susceptible to these winds. As well, personal preference and family needs play a role. For example, eleusine, or finger millet, is widely consumed by infants, so a farmer with an especially young family might well plant more of it. According to Netting, "It is this series of modifications, of delicate adjustments to varying environments, which most clearly attests to Kofyar agricultural skill."[41]

But Kofyar agricultural prowess is not limited to these practices. Restricted to their refuge fields and with little land available for expansion or for leaving fallow, the Kofyar focus on sustaining the productivity of their homestead fields. This is achieved partly through careful crop mixes — for example, both cowpeas and groundnuts being used to fix nitrogen — but most obviously through constant manuring and fertilizing. Every household keeps chickens and goats, the latter in a stone corral near the household. Green leaves and brush are provided both as fodder and as a base for the corral; they get mixed with goat urine and manure. Household ash is added, and the resultant mix

provides a rich organic base for crops. In some locales with particularly restricted land, night soil is also added. As Netting says, "for nine months of the
year every available bit of manure is retained."[42] The result is homestead fields
that have remained remarkably productive, year after year, for generations.

The Kofyar are equally careful about work. Crop mixes are not attuned
simply to soil, wind, water and wants but are also calibrated to require
seeding and harvesting at different times of the year and by different
groups within the household. Though such intensive agriculture requires
significantly more labour per acre than any other form of farming, household
labour is spread throughout the year and there is little need to hire from
outside the family.

Also, despite colonial administrators dismayed by what they perceived as
a stagnant traditionalism in West Africa among peasant cultivators resistant
to "ordering" by colonial officials and reluctant to mechanize, the Kofyar
readily integrated new crops and techniques. Netting reported that a new
maize type that predominated at the time of his field work in the 1960s had
been in use for less than two decades. And as the opportunity to expand
to areas on the base of plateau arose in the middle of the 20th century, the
Kofyar added bushland to the homestead plots. Here they engaged in different agricultural techniques. Using more land, unrestricted by the land
shortages in the homestead fields and conscious of the limits to available
labour that would allow intensive agriculture, they let some land lie fallow
rather than engage in intensive manuring of the homestead. Even here,
however, they employed careful techniques to maintain the fertility of their
land. For example, they provided inducements to Fulani herdsmen to camp
temporarily on their land to take advantage of the dung from their herds.
Kofyar resisted entreaties from colonial administrators and development
experts to change their agricultural practices, use more mechanization
and specialize production for the market. They did so not out of stubborn
resistance to change but because such changes would have threatened the
continued viability of their fields and their livelihoods.

The Kofyar are not a population bound by tradition to ever-decreasing
agricultural returns. Rather, they are a people who built culture, community
and abundance out of difficult terrain. Two and a half acres of homestead garden provided a family of five with reasonable subsistence. Palm oil, canarium
oil and browncakes made from locust bean were sold in the markets, along
with other crops from homestead and bush fields. As Netting comments,
despite the inhibitions forced on them by outside forces, "Their mastery of
their environment was such that hunger was rare and serious famine was
known only in legend."[43]

"Inventive Self-Reliance"

Writing in 1985, Paul Richards argued that "inventive self-reliance is one of Africa's most precious resources." Like Serge Latouche, he suggested it could be found most readily in West African peasants.[44] John Berger, the noted historian of peasant life, once told Michael Watts that, "what is talked about in our world normally covers so little of what is being lived in the world that surrounds us."[45] Though more than a century of writing on West Africa has portrayed that region's agriculturalists as the main culprits in an ongoing demographic and environmental catastrophe, those who explored such smallholder agriculture more closely were very often singularly impressed. Polycropped fields used land and labour in West Africa more efficiently and to greater effect than any of the proffered modern solutions. Polycropping proved more effective than mechanized large-scale agriculture or even a green revolution dependent on hybrid seeds and chemical inputs, which would transfer human food into animal feed. West African peasants resisted demands to adopt new crops, new technologies and new activities. This was not out of some hidebound resistance to change. Rather, it was because such change could not fit into the complex and intricate agricultural system that provided the basis for Kofyar community, culture and careful abundance.

NOTES

1   See Robin Blackburn, *The Making of New World Slavery: From the Baroque to the Modern, 1492–1800,* London: Verso, 1997, 152; John Thornton, *Africa and Africans in the Making of the Atlantic World, 1400–1800,* Cambridge: Cambridge University Press, 1992.

2   *Economist,* "Free Trade and Slave Trade," 1:10 (Nov. 4, 1843), 156; *Economist,* "The Slave Trade and Slavery — Mr. Hutt's Motion," 3:26 (June 28, 1845), 597–598; *Economist,* "Can the Slave Trade Be Suppressed," 6:262 (Sept. 2, 1848), 993–995.

3   James McCann, *Green Land, Brown Land, Black Land: An Environmental History of Africa, 1800–1990,* Portsmouth, NH: Heinemann, 1999; Melissa Leach and James Fairhead, *Misreading the African Landscape: Society and Ecology in a Forest-Savanna Mosaic,* Cambridge: Cambridge University Press, 1996; Melissa Leach and Robert Mearns (eds.), *The Lie of the Land: Challenging Received Wisdom on the African Environment,* Oxford: James Currey Ltd. 1996; especially Jeremy Swift, "Desertification: Narratives, Winners and Losers," in Leach and Mearns, *The Lie of the Land,* 1996; Roy H. Benke and Michael Mortimore (eds.), *The End of Desertification? Disputing Environmental Change in the Drylands,* Berlin: Springer-Verlag, 2016.

4   Cited in Roland Littlewood, "Jungle Madness: Some Observations on Expatriate Psychopathology," *International Journal of Social Psychiatry* 9:31 (1985), 3.

5   Garret Hardin, "The Tragedy of the Commons," *Science* 162: 3859 (Dec. 1968),

1243–1248.

6   Paul Ehrlich, *The Population Bomb: Population Control or Race to Oblivion?* San Francisco: Sierra Club, 1968; Donella H. Meadows et al., *Limits to Growth,* Washington, DC: Potomac Associates, 1972; Garret Hardin, "Living on a Lifeboat," *BioScience* 24:10 (1974), 561–568.

7   Robert Kaplan, "The Coming Anarchy: How Scarcity, Crime, Overpopulation and Disease are Rapidly Destroying the Social Fabric of our Planet," *The Atlantic,* Feb. 1994, 44–76.

8   Thomas Homer-Dixon, *Environment, Scarcity, and Violence,* Princeton: Princeton University Press, 1999.

9   Roderick Neumann, *Imposing Wilderness: Struggles over Livelihood and Nature Preservation in Africa,* Berkeley: University of California Press, 2002.

10 Ester Boserup, *Economic and Demographic Relationships in Development* (ed. T. Paul Schultz), Baltimore: Johns Hopkins University Press, 1990, esp. 26, 39.

11 *Economist,* "African Cotton and Cotton Manufactures in Relation to the Slave Trade," 17:810 (March 5, 1859), 251–253; *Economist,* "English Feelings Toward America," 19:944 (Sept. 28, 1861), 1065–1067.

12 Crawford Young, *The African Colonial State in Comparative Perspective,* New Haven: Yale University Press, 1994.

13 Paul Lovejoy, "Plantations in the Economy of the Sokoto Caliphate," *The Journal of African History* 19:3 (1978), 341–368.

14 Michael Watts, *Silent Violence: Food, Famine and Peasantry in Northern Nigeria,* Athens, Georgia: University of Georgia Press, 2013 [1983], esp. 61–113.

15 Young, *The African Colonial State,* 1994, 179; Mahmood Mamdani, *Citizen and Subject: Contemporary Africa and the Legacy of Late Colonialism,* Princeton: Princeton University Press, 2018, esp. 148–165.

16 Watts, *Silent Violence,* 2013, 258.

17 Ibid., 303.

18 Cited in Paul Richards, *Indigenous Agricultural Revolution: Ecology and Food Production in West Africa,* London: Hutchinson, 1985, 30.

19 Ibid., 35.

20 Watts, *Silent Violence,* 2013, 336.

21 Kavita Philip, *Civilizing Natures: Race, Resources, and Modernity in Colonial South India,* New Brunswick, New Jersey: Rutgers, 2004, 7.

22 Richards, *Indigenous Agricultural Revolution,* 1985, 35.

23 Goran Hyden, *Beyond Ujamaa in Tanzania: Underdevelopment and an Uncaptured Peasantry,* Berkeley: University of California Press, 1980, 31.

24 Keith Hart, *The Political Economy of West African Agriculture,* Cambridge: Cambridge University Press, 1982, 83–84.

25 W.A. Lewis, "Economic Development with Unlimited Supplies of Labour," in A.N. Agarwala and S.P. Singh (eds.), *The Economics of Underdevelopment,* Oxford: Oxford University Press, 1958, esp. 408, 448, 434.

26 John Cleave, *African Farmers: Labor Use in the Development of Smallholder Agriculture,* New York: Praeger Publishers, 1974, 1, 13.

27 Richards, *Indigenous Agricultural Revolution,* 1985, 123–124.

28 Mikael Bergius and Jill Tove Buseth "Towards a Green Modernization

Development Discourse: the New Green Revolution in Africa," *Journal of Political Ecology* 26 (2019), 57–83.

29 For various critiques of proposals for a green revolution in Africa, see Abdallah Ramadhani Mkindi et al., *False Promises: The Alliance for a Green Revolution in Africa (AGRA)*, various international publishers, https://grain.org/en/article/6499-false-promises-the-alliance-for-a-green-revolution-in-africa-agra, 2020; Eric Holt-Giménez, "Out of AGRA: The Green Revolution Returns to Africa," *Development* 51 (2008), 464–471; Peter Lawrence, "The Political Economy of the 'Green Revolution' in Africa," *Review of African Political Economy*, 15:42 (1988), 59–75; Elenita C. Daño, "Unmasking the Green Revolution in Africa," *Rural 21* (2008), 32–36; Timothy Wise, "Failing Africa's Farmers: An Impact Assessment of the Alliance for a Green Revolution in Africa," *Global Development and Environment Institute, Working Paper 20-01,* Tufts University (July 2020).

30 Xinshen Diao, Derek Headey and Michael Johnson, "Toward a Green Revolution in Africa: What Would It Achieve, and What Would It Require? *Agricultural Economics* 39, supplement (2008), 539–550.

31 William Kerr, "Food Sovereignty — Old Protectionism in Somewhat Recycled Bottles," *African Technology and Development Forum Journal* 8 (2011), 4–9.

32 Serge Latouche, *In the Wake of the Affluent Society: An Exploration of Post-Development,* London: Zed Press, 1993. (Originally published in French as *La Planète des Naufragés: essai sur l'après-développement,* La Découverte: Paris, 1991.)

33 See for example the chapters in Sylviane Diouf (ed.), *Fighting the Slave Trade: West African Strategies,* Athens, Ohio: Ohio University Press, 2003; Paul Lovejoy, "Slavery in the Sokoto Caliphate," in Lovejoy (ed.), *The Ideology of Slavery in Africa,* Beverly Hills: Sage Publications, 1981, 201–243.

34 A.G. Hopkins, *An Economic History of West Africa,* London: Longman Group Ltd., 1973, esp. 31.

35 Richards, *Indigenous Agricultural Revolution,* 1985, 63.

36 Matt Liebman, "Polyculture Cropping Systems," in Miguel Altieri et al., *Agroecology: The Science of Sustainable Agriculture,* Boulder: Westview Press, 1987, 205–217.

37 Boserup, *Economic and Demographic Relationships,* 1990, 47.

38 Richards, *Indigenous Agricultural Revolution,* 1985, 68.

39 Liebman, "Polyculture Cropping Systems," 1987, 217.

40 The following discussion draws from Robert McC. Netting, *Hill Farmers of Nigeria: Cultural Ecology of the Kofyar of the Jos Plateau,* Seattle: University of Washington Press, 1968. Netting provided some updates in a much shorter discussion of the Kofyar in *Smallholders, Householders: Farm Families and the Ecology of Intensive, Sustainable Agriculture,* Stanford: Stanford University Press, 1993.

41 Netting, *Hill Farmers,* 1968, 77.

42 Netting, *Hill Farmers,* 1968, 61–62.

43 Netting, *Hill Farmers,* 1968, 5.

44 Richards, *Indigenous Agricultural Revolution,* 1985, 16.

45 Cited in Watts, *Silent Violence,* 2013, ixxiii.

KERALA

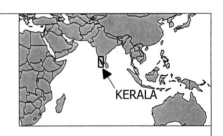

KERALA

Elevation

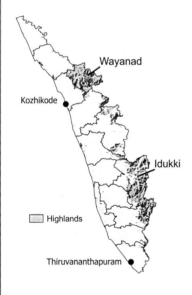

Wayanad

Kozhikode

Idukki

☐ Highlands

Thiruvananthapuram

Princely States

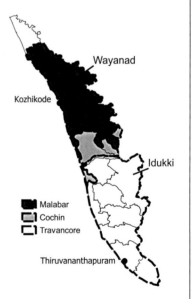

Wayanad

Kozhikode

Idukki

■ Malabar
☐ Cochin
☐ Travancore

Thiruvananthapuram

6 Kerala: A Return to the Future

As I write this chapter, Indian farmers are protesting government plans to end marketing supports for a wide range of basic crops. Hundreds of thousands of small farmers, women and children among them, braved the COVID-19 pandemic and government harassment in an attempt to maintain price supports they believed necessary for their survival as farmers. This widespread protest occurred following decades of falling rural incomes, farmers being squeezed between escalating costs of inputs and declining prices. For these farmers, life is so precarious that it prompts thousands to commit suicide every year, many through the symbolic but grisly act of swallowing a particularly deadly and common pesticide, either Sulfas or Furadan.[1]

The Indian state of Kerala is one of those caught in the throes of declining rural incomes and farmer suicides. This is surprising because Kerala, a small state in the southwest of India, was the site of ongoing reforms beginning almost immediately after its formation in 1956. Despite opposition from the central government and some false starts, coalition governments in Kerala implemented various rounds of agrarian reforms. These reforms, coupled with protection for labour, significant social spending on basic health care, high levels of education, a vibrant political culture, and widespread civil society and co-operative organizations fostered a series of beneficial changes in Kerala. Despite low income levels, by the 1980s the state boasted a range of health and social indicators — health status, infant mortality rates, life expectancy and education levels — that were more favourable than many other countries with a much higher GDP per capita. Most remarkable, perhaps, were statistics indicating women's access to education and health care and their ability to make decisions about family planning. These accomplishments were so impressive that many commentators, both from India and elsewhere, extolled the virtues of what became known as the Kerala model of development, one that seemed to promise a good life without the need to wait until a rising tide of increased GDP lifted all.

Much of the shine has worn off the Kerala model. Despite more than fifty years of reform, the results, at least by some economic measures, have been disappointing. Unemployment is widespread and agricultural production has not increased as some had hoped. Before COVID restricted movement, a high percentage of labourers left Kerala for the Gulf States. Their remittances formed an increasingly important part of family economy, and by the early 1990s, made up more than 13 percent of Kerala's GDP.[2] And despite agrarian reform, hundreds of farmers in Kerala ended desperate lives by intentionally drinking pesticide. Indeed, Kerala ranked near the top of Indian states for farmer suicides as a percentage of the population.[3]

What went wrong? Was the Kerala model of development simply a chimera, never a model and never sustainable? And how is Kerala's fall from grace linked to our survey of peasant agriculture around the world and over time? This chapter argues that the Kerala model of development was and is real, and that truly beneficial development can occur without a fixation on growth. Inadequate income certainly plays a part in Kerala's ongoing difficulties. But despite land and labour reforms, the problems that lie at the heart of the region's struggles resemble those explored elsewhere in this book. Despite reforms, significant amounts of land were left in large-scale plantations. In many communities, elite castes were able to dominate landholding despite the legal provisions in the reform laws. Most importantly, government policy failed to take advantage of the very real strengths and efficiencies of smallholder agriculture in Kerala, most apparent in the productivity of house gardens associated with hutdwellers' benefits gained in the 1969 Land Reform Amendment Act.

As the green revolution washed over India in earnest in the 1970s, Kerala's farmers were encouraged to follow the same path: chasing returns from cash crops; buying into green revolution promises of high yields and profits despite increased expenditures and the debt and environmental problems that accompanied green revolution varieties and technology. While hutdwellers benefited from laws that gave them secure tenure in their tiny house garden plots, they too were encouraged by government policy and by the lack of alternatives to focus on simplified agriculture or permaculture. These approaches increased cash income but failed to provide the diverse range of products for domestic use that traditional house gardens could and did. They too began to depend on a mix of pesticides and expensive inputs. Very recently, governments in Kerala have sought to reverse some of these policies, promote organic agriculture, ban chemical pesticides and fertilizers, and belatedly, tap into the potential advantages of multicropping in intensive cultivation. It is early days in this transformation, but results are promising. Given the history of peasant innovation and abundance we have explored in previous chapters, these results should not surprise us.

A Caste-Riven State

Kerala was created in 1956 by pasting together two princely states, Travancore and Cochin, and the former British colony of Malabar, part of the Madras Presidency. Though their histories diverged, the three parts of Kerala are linked through a common language, Malayalam, broadly similar caste divisions and populations, with about 80 percent Hindu, 10 percent Muslim and 10 percent Christian.

The British East India Company and later colonial rulers recognized princely states in order to control regions and populations within India without the bother of governing. Many commentators suggested that princely states were the worst possible form of rule: the ruling dynasties had no real power and little real authority despite their official positions.[4] Nonetheless, Travancore in particular was a reasonably well-run entity before independence. As the state expanded its territory in the late 18th and early 19th centuries, it took over areas controlled by Nair headmen. Partly to curb their power, the princely rulers gave headmen's tenants fixed tenure on the land with relatively low taxation levels. By the mid-19th century, these tenants were given full ownership of their land. They did not cultivate land directly but relied on dependent labourers, most often determined by caste position. In the decades leading up to independence and immediately afterwards, before being joined along with others to form the state of Kerala, Travancore also expanded education and provided a widespread school meal program.[5]

Malabar, as a direct colony of the British, suffered a different fate. Land policy under the British East India Company varied throughout the country. In Malabar, the British colonial state assumed that Kerala's Brahmins, called Namboordiripads, who made up less than 2 percent of the population, enjoyed essentially absolute ownership over the land rather than the complicated customary control tradition dictated.[6]

Throughout the state, agriculture has always been deeply interwoven with caste inequalities. Land was typically "owned" by a very small group of upper caste Brahmins who leased large parcels of land to Nair or occasionally to Christian tenants. Before 1969, landlords in Kerala might have been able to demand a higher percentage of the crop than in almost any other location in Asia. One study in 1948 demonstrated that tenants were forced to provide up to 90 percent of the harvest to pay for land.[7] These upper caste tenants did not cultivate the land but rather relied on lower caste or Muslim tenants, who in turn often relied on even lower caste Pulayas to work the land. Workers (hutdwellers or *kudikidappukars*) held their huts along with very small amounts of land around their residences on insecure tenure and faced the constant threat of eviction. Such pressure helped ensure dependent and quiescent labourers.[8]

Nonetheless, in Malabar in particular, serious agrarian uprisings occurred throughout the 19th century and into the 20th. In 1921, a group of mostly Muslim tenants rose in what is called the Mappila Rebellion, during which 10,000 people, including more than 600 Hindu landlords, were killed.[9] Building on these tensions, the Communist Party formed in 1939 and helped spark the growth of the Kerala Peasants' Union, which had 190,000 members by 1957.

Some very specific conflicts over land occurred in the eastern districts of what became the state of Kerala. The British viewed the hill districts of the western Ghats, especially those that became the Wayanad and Idukki regions, as propitious terrain for the development of plantation crops, particularly coffee and tea, under the control of European colonists. Dominance over these forested regions was thought to be a necessary expression of mastery over particularly problematic colonial subjects. British administrators portrayed the inhabitants of forests as more barbaric and less evolved than more settled populations engaged in different types of cultivation. The purported deficiencies of the indigenous population allowed administrators to extol the benefits of European-controlled coffee, tea and cinchona plantations, with the intent of civilizing both the forest and its inhabitants.[10] As a result, the eastern hill districts of Malabar were tied early to the production of a range of cash crops, notably tea, pepper and coffee.

Land Reform

It is not surprising that struggles around land became important soon after the state of Kerala was created in 1956. The first elected government of the new state, led by the Communist Party with its base in labour unions and the Kerala Peasants' Union, almost immediately passed the Land Reform Act of 1957. The state government was heatedly opposed by a coalition of a socialist party, the state Congress Party and the All-India Muslim League in what they termed a "democratic unity against totalitarianism." This coalition worked assiduously to portray the government as a prelude to a totalitarian takeover and fostered widespread opposition involving sometimes violent demonstrations and tactics designed to make it impossible to govern the state. After a two-day visit there, President Jawaharlal Nehru declared that the state was on the verge of a mass uprising and the administration unable to maintain law and order. The Communist government was dismissed after twenty-eight months in power and presidential rule imposed. The Land Reform Act was later declared unconstitutional.[11]

This was an ignoble end to the first Communist-led government in India, but it had lasting effects on Kerala. In the 1960s, the Communist Party split into the Communist Party of India and the Communist Party Marxist. Since then, state power has oscillated between a Congress-led coalition (sometimes with a socialist party as a major player) and a left coalition led by the most powerful of the communist parties. Communist Party-led coalitions — United or Left Democratic Fronts — were in power again in the late 1960s through much of the 1970s, back for a while in the mid-1980s, in 1996, from 2006–2011 and again in 2016. When in power, they have most often enacted major social, land or agrarian legislation. Even when they are not in power, however, the vibrant social, peasant and worker organizations that typify politics in Kerala ensure that even more conservative coalitions headed by the Congress Party are forced to legislate land and worker reforms.

Following the reversal of the 1957 Land Reform Act, the Congress government passed a moderate agrarian reform in 1963. This was dramatically strengthened in 1969 when the Kerala Land Reforms Amendment Act was passed. Though some significant agrarian reform bills have been passed since, most commentators point to the 1969 act as the decisive break in Kerala agriculture and one of the key ingredients in what became known as the Kerala model of development. Ronald Herring argued that the decade that followed "compressed a remarkable span of history into a short span of years. New property rights were established, old ones extinguished; novel property-like rights and obligations were created, distributed, and then redistributed."[12] The law had four major components: a rice tax on large landowners to provide the poor with subsidized rice, an absolute ceiling of ten acres on the size of holdings with the exception of some plantation crops, the abolition of tenancy to non-cultivating landlords, and the provision to *kudikidappukaran* of secure ownership of huts and one tenth of an acre of land surrounding the hut.

The first two components of the law were never successfully implemented. Worried about both rice production for domestic consumption and export earnings, the state left large amounts of land in large-scale plantations for a range of crops — rice, tea, coconuts — and numerous studies have shown that locally privileged elites were able relatively quickly to concentrate land ownership after the reforms. But the other two aspects of the reform proved critical. By the early 1990s, almost three million tenants had become landowners. Perhaps most importantly, more than five million people, many of them agricultural labourers or hutdwellers, gained ownership rights over their huts and small amounts of land. The significance of these changes is more fully discussed below.[13]

Equally as important as the actual redistribution of rights and land accompanying this agrarian reform was the way such land struggles spurred dynamic social and popular organizations in the state. The passage of the amendment in 1969, and the mostly successful efforts to ensure that some of the provisions of the law were implemented in the years to follow, helped Kerala earn a reputation for political agitation and social activism. While this meant the state was often considered politically "problematic," this vibrancy was an essential component of the Kerala model of development.[14]

The Kerala Model?

The Kerala difference — the way the state was able to offer many of the important measures of a good life in the absence of increased income levels — has been widely discussed. By 1994, Kerala had adult literacy and life expectancy rates that were dramatically better than India's as a whole and that approximated those of the richest countries in the world. The adult literacy rate was above 90 percent (the UN declared it to have, in effect, a 100 percent literacy rate), and life expectancy was 69 years for men and 72 for women. The GNP per capita in Brazil and South Africa was many times that of Kerala, with life expectancy at birth 10 years shorter. Infant mortality and birth rates were remarkably lower in Kerala than for India as whole, and were startlingly lower than other locales in the world where income levels per capita were significantly higher. Not only did Kerala do better in these indices than India as a whole, but it compared favourably and improved faster than almost all of the fastest- growing Asian economies. In 1991, the United Nations placed Kerala's Physical Quality of Life Index, a measure of incomes and other factors of importance, at 88, which was slightly higher than South Korea's despite a significantly lower income and which eclipsed the rating of 66 for the rest of India.

The state had reduced its birth rate to levels similar to the richest countries of the world, without resorting to any of the forced or violent measures implemented elsewhere with less success.[15] Perhaps most startlingly, Kerala reversed the missing woman syndrome apparent elsewhere in India and many other countries in Asia. In India in 2001, there were 933 women for every 1,000 men, an imbalance resulting from systemic violence against girls and women and their inability to command resources necessary to survive. In Kerala, there were 1,058 women to every 1,000 males, a figure approximating the natural tendency of women to live longer than men.[16] Kerala had done all of this despite a stubbornly low income per capita, at about 70 percent of the already low Indian average, and with 740 people per hectare, being one of the most densely populated places on earth.[17]

Kerala's citizens have access to a dynamic press and public debate. The state has a remarkable level of community organization and numerous co-operatives. While it hasn't completely avoided the sectarian violence occurring in many others states in India, it is less apparent in Kerala. Further, the current national governing party, the Bharatiya Janata Party, which has its roots in a sometimes violent Hindu nationalism, does poorly in state elections.

For many observers in the 1980s and early 1990s, Kerala's remarkable successes suggested that it might serve as a model for genuine social development without the fixation on economic growth. Writing near the end of the 1990s, Patrick Heller argued that the reforms in Kerala were "arguably the most successful strategy of redistributive development outside the socialist world." Earlier in the decade, Richard Franke and Barbara Chasin remarked: "Kerala offers an alternative ... in place of cuts in services to assuage foreign investors, instead of growing inequality, and the deterioration or collapse of secular government, Kerala's planners and villagers are attempting to create genuine participation, empowerment, equality, reasonable self-reliance, and concern for the environment that could lead to sustainable development."[18] And in 1996, a report for the Institute for Food and Development Policy argued: "Kerala demonstrates that a low-level economy can create a decent life, abundant in the things — health, education, community — that are most necessary for us all."[19]

A Model in Shambles

And yet, many commentators have argued strenuously that Kerala can provide no models. As T.G. Jacob most vehemently expresses it, "Very soon, the so-called model was exposed as a sham! ... By the mid-1990s, the model was thoroughly debunked!"[20] While Jacob uses more exclamation points in his assessment, many others have expressed serious reservations about Kerala's development.

Criticisms of the Kerala experience point to some common concerns. The state's inability to couple such reforms with increased economic growth is tied to worries about high unemployment rates and increased government debt. There are constant complaints about the efficiency of agriculture in Kerala. The agricultural sector is said to be stagnant, with falling production and reduced income from cash crops. All of this has meant that agriculture provides a smaller percentage of the state's GDP than it did in the 1950s, when the land reform was initiated.

As we will see below, these concerns must be approached with a degree of caution and put into context. There is no denying some of Kerala's most obvious economic failures. Kerala's unenviable record of the third-highest rate of farmer suicides per capita and an increasing percentage of its population, mostly young people, seeking work in the Gulf States are eloquent testimony to some of those failures. It is thus worth taking seriously these multiple criticisms of the Kerala model of development and exploring to what extent they might be related to the type of agricultural policies followed in Kerala, despite its vaunted land reforms.

Certainly, increases in Kerala's official GDP have not always kept pace with other Indian states. In 1970, official per capita GDP in Kerala was 93 percent of the Indian average. By the 1990s, this had fallen to 70 percent. Even some of those who expressed admiration for what Kerala was able to accomplish, like the economist Amartya Sen, worry about the state's inability to raise the GDP. Others are more critical, perhaps Joseph Tharamangalam and K.K. George most notably. Tharamangalam coined the term the "development debacle" in an influential article in the *Bulletin of Concerned Asian Scholars* in 1998 to raise the alarm about Kerala's failings. Warning about the "perils of social development without economic growth," he cited a litany of problems confronting Kerala and argued that the state was "in the throes of a major fiscal, economic, political, and cultural crisis." Tharamangalam and others stressed declining employment in both agriculture and industry, suggesting that artificially heightened wages (through labour legislation or unionization rather than market demand) meant that many traditional industries in Kerala had moved elsewhere. Further, as a consequence of reduced government income and continued high social expenditures, the state government was deeply in debt, with little relief on the horizon.[21]

Critics occasionally point to external causes for these multiple crises. An example is the role that temporary labour migration to the Gulf States and remittances as a form of "Dutch Disease" plays in driving up the price of labour beyond the point where it can be employed profitably.[22] But what is most often attacked in such works is the way that the various agrarian reforms, especially the application of the 1969 Land Reform Amendment Act, led to a myriad of problems for Kerala agriculture. This requires some careful exploration.

Criticisms of Kerala's agricultural economy in the decades following the 1969 Land Reform Amendment Act usually focus on specific concerns: the supposed stagnation of agricultural production as a whole; a decline in the production of rice; an increased dependence on food from outside the state of Kerala; and the reduction in the percentage of the population engaged in agriculture. Critics are prone to link these supposed problems with the success of the reform itself. They claim that land was given out to too many small farmers to such an extent that the farms are no longer capable of sustaining a family, are inefficient and are forcing many people from the land — a replication of the Malthusian argument.

It is certainly true that the 1969 Amendment provided land to many small farmers, both former tenants and hutdwellers. More than 80 percent of the landholdings in Kerala are less than an acre.[23] These smallholdings are linked to numerous problems, according to analysts. They have led to decreased incomes for farming families and to the apparent unproductiveness of agriculture as a whole. Only about 12 percent of Kerala's population now claims to make the bulk of its income from agricultural production, while labour costs have increased and agriculture profits declined.[24]

Of much concern is the decline in paddy rice production, the major foodstuff in the state. Kerala has never been self-sufficient in rice production. However, following disruption of the usual distribution networks for rice accompanying the Second World War, there was a major push to produce more rice in the region. In the 1960s and early 1970s, substantial subsidies were provided to rice producers, and the state, though not self-sufficient, met more of its basic food needs. This was especially true as both the state and national governments pushed green revolution technology focused, in this region, on rice production. However, by the 1970s, artificially stimulated rice prices declined with the removal of subsidies, and between 1967 and 2004, rice-growing acreage fell from 48 percent of the total area in food crops to 10 percent.[25]

Concerns about rice production seem exaggerated. Much of the decline in rice acreage was the result of decisions by smallholders about the most profitable or most productive crop mix on small plots of land. Except in some special wetland regions, rice production is not the most profitable nor most sustainable use of land in Kerala. With the removal of artificial stimulus to rice prices, smallholders, especially those holding very small bits of land, moved out of rice production to a mix of perennial and annual crops that provided them much higher returns. Some perennial crops, like rubber, could produce five times the income per acre compared to rice.[26] Other perennial crops allowed for a more diverse and robust mix than rice paddy agriculture and could foster a better apportioning of labour time.

It is certainly true that the freeing of hutdwellers entailed in the Land Reform Amendment Act provided options to millions of the poorest rural inhabitants. It is also true that these options included holding out for higher wages or even leaving rural areas for jobs in industry or tourism or in the Gulf States. But even the most severe critics of Kerala's model would not argue that such freedom was, on balance, negative, or that a reasonable response would be to end that freedom, though at least one critic has defined that freedom as "alienating the beneficiary from the existing labouring agreement."[27] Indeed, the whole discussion about labour shortage in agriculture in Kerala seems overblown, while it is clear that labour at prices large farmers would like to pay is in short supply.

Moreover, there is serious doubt about whether there has in fact been a decline in agricultural production in Kerala, and if so, what has caused this. Many of the critics who expressed alarm at declining production seem to have been keen to find this as the expected outcome of the "radical" agrarian reform of the Kerala Communist Party governments. Many carefully chose statistics from specific years to prove this.[28] Instead, though the mix of agriculture products and the amount of agricultural production that was destined for the market or for home consumption changed over time, it appears agricultural production as a whole increased in Kerala from the 1960s through to the middle of the 1970s. It declined after that until the early 1980s but reversed course and has increased since then.[29] Though these increases have not kept pace with production in some other states in India, this is primarily a function of Kerala's small land base and alternative options for labour elsewhere. They are also linked to the long-term negative effects of green revolution inputs. Even Joseph Tharamangalam, perhaps the most noted critic of the Kerala experience, has admitted that much of Kerala's economic decline is more apparent than real — a function of the invisibility in economic accounts of remittances — and that "real per capita income … is almost certainly higher than the Indian average," and not 73 percent of that average, as the GDP figures would suggest. [30]

The Green Havoc

There is no denying the crises, both individual and more generalized, that prompted some farmers to seek a final solution through Furadan. To understand how this is related to small-scale peasant agriculture, we need to put the lives of those desperate farmers into context. To do this, we need to explore the limitations of Kerala's agrarian reform and some of the contemporary ramifications of those limitations. We also need to understand more fully the cost/price squeeze many farmers in India felt as a result of the combined effects of neoliberal restructuring and the long-term implications of the adoption of green revolution technology.

Kerala's agrarian reform, beginning in 1969, was one of the most significant and important reforms in Asia in the 20th century, "snapp[ing] the centuries-old feudal strings" that tied tenants and labourers to landlords through the privileges afforded upper caste Brahmins, in the words of P. Radhakrishnan.[31] But it left much undone. Policies exempting plantation crops from the cap on size meant much of the land seized from forest-dwellers in the colonial period, especially in the Wayanad and Idukki districts, was never redistributed. This left the door open for plantations to expand through various forms of land accumulation in the years following, despite the intent of the reform. In early 2000, a single plantation controlled 25,000 hectares of land; various governments have found it difficult or have been unwilling to recover the land such plantations control.[32] This has restricted severely the amount of land that can be distributed to landless or land poor labourers.

In addition, while the reform effectively ended rapacious forms of tenancy agreements that tied small farmers renting plots to upper caste landlords, in many regions a free market in buying or leasing land has meant that those with significant capital or non-farm income have been able to buy up land. These processes helped reconfigure land ownership in some communities, shifting it from the traditional elite castes and benefiting either the more commercially oriented tenants or the members of elite castes who had obtained well-paid professional positions and could plough money back into land. In the process, the commoditization of land ensured that landless and land-poor labourers in many villages were unable to get access.[33]

Without a doubt, the most important and beneficial aspect of the 1969 reform was providing hutdwellers secure ownership of their huts and the house gardens surrounding them. In some districts this also included a small portion of intensely used permaculture forest land. Relieving hutdwellers from the threat of expulsion from their homes and properties was a major step in permitting their fuller participation in politics and activist movements — without endangering their homes. In this sense, this part of the reform was an essential step in rural development, providing hutdwellers with a "defensible life space," which John Friedmann argued was the necessary first step in real development.[34] As we will see below, hutdwellers with secure tenure, like those holding tiny bits of land in the other places we have examined, were often able to make these small parcels remarkably productive through intensive polyculture. Their ability to turn them into tiny engines of abundance was constrained by two things: the diminishing size of these bits of land — given the failure of the agrarian reforms to effectively enforce the cap on holdings and distribute more land — and the fascination of various governments in Kerala with the promise of the green revolution. Let's turn to the latter concern first.

As we have seen in the various chapters of this book, one of the most enduring aspects of the fairy dust of political economy that hung over the agricultural revolution in late 18th- and early 19th-century England was the argument put forward by the Reverend Thomas Robert Malthus. He warned that unless the poor were made to feel the results of their reckless propagation through increased wretchedness, they would happily overpopulate the earth. This was always the most arresting and influential part of Malthus's legacy, never far from the surface of much modern thought. Malthus was also exercised about the potential for unrest among the poor. He argued that if the "great truths" about the poor creating their own poverty through having too many children were widely known, "the greatest part of the mischievous declamation on the unjust institutions of society would fall powerless to the ground."[35]

Malthus spent most of his adult life as the first professor of General History, Politics, Commerce and Finance at the East India Company College, where all would-be mid-level administrators for the company were trained. From 1805, when he was first appointed at the college, to his death in 1834, he provided these young men with five lectures a week on the proper ordering of societies. Malthus's warning about the multiple dangers that resulted from peasants having access to land, and thus easy subsistence for their families, helped shape British policy in India. The image of India that emerged, as a place hindered by too many people pressing too hard on the land, remained after Indian independence. This perception was important in India's embrace of the green revolution.

The green revolution was the result of US scientists', governments' and business interests' fascination with the potential for increased harvests of foodstuffs using the right mix of engineered plants and technological inputs. The basic component, at least of early green revolution technology, was engineering high-yield dwarf varieties of food crops (notably corn, wheat and rice) that were amenable to nitrogen-based fertilizers first developed for corn in the US Midwest. And just as Malthus was much concerned with the potential for unrest among the poor, the spread of green revolution technology was always seen as an essential element in the fight against communism. These components were translated to an international venture, one of the cornerstones of the US government's announced dedication to "development," when the vice-president-elect, secretary of agriculture and owner of Pioneer-Hybrid (all one person), Henry Wallace, convinced Avila Comacho at the latter's inauguration in 1940 to invite American scientists to Mexico to help develop hybrid corn varieties. This was done partly to strengthen Camacho's turn away from the "dangerous" agrarian populism of former President Lázaro Cárdenas.[36]

New hybrid varieties of corn had limited success in Mexico, but the technology was soon expanded to other major food staples and transported elsewhere. India, with its image as a place of teaming populations, too little land and at constant risk of embracing communism, was a natural venue for such agricultural Cold War dreams.

US officials met some resistance there. K. M. Munshi, the first minister of agriculture after independence, was an admirer of Gandhi and argued that India needed better to harness the natural processes in its villages. Despite Munshi's appeal, the country soon turned into a grand theatre for the unfolding of the green revolution. Munshi was replaced by the former minister of steel and heavy industry, Chidambara Subramaniam, who was an ardent supporter of science applied to agriculture generally and green revolution technology specifically. Any hesitancy was swept aside when in the aftermath of war with Pakistan and in the midst of a severe drought. President Lyndon Johnson tied US food aid to India to acceptance of green revolution technology. Its promise was eagerly embraced by Indira Gandhi, who was similarly worried about the increase in (certain) sectors of the Indian population and hoped the adoption of green revolution technology would help make her version of authoritarian agrarian populism more acceptable without the need for massive agrarian reform.[37]

As its proponents promised, high-yield varieties of wheat increased production in parts of India, helping to end reliance on Plan 480 food aid from the US and feed its increasing populations as it industrialized. But production and rice yields across India actually increased at a slower pace after the introduction of green revolution technologies than in the decade before. The increases in wheat production were probably more often the result of access to water through intensive development of tube wells than of any change in crop varieties or seeds.[38]

The limited increase in production came at a cost. High-yield varieties required much more water than "traditional" ones, spurring both huge costs and dislocations as India desperately sought more water for irrigation through dams and lost agricultural land through salination caused by excessive irrigation. They also required huge chemical inputs. In Uttar Pradesh, for example, it is estimated that chemical fertilizer use mushroomed from six kilos per acre in the mid-1960s to more than a hundred kilos per acre by the 1980s. This made some — though limited — economic sense as long as agricultural prices were high and the cost of such chemical inputs low. However, by the middle of the 1980s, as higher petroleum prices drove input prices higher, agricultural prices also declined. This decline was sharpened by the withdrawal of subsidies for agricultural products mandated by neoliberal restructuring. Monocropping, widespread pesticide and chemical fertilizer use and extensive irrigation associated with such crops led to widespread environmental problems. Inequality increased as the smallest farm units were deprived of necessary inputs (for example, access to water from tube wells or irrigation available to wealthier farmers). Yields declined as the land deteriorated or as impoverished farmers could not afford to maintain chemical inputs. And many farmers, especially the small and marginal, fell into a deepening debt trap.[39]

Kerala's agriculture was also caught in the maelstrom. The state's reform government in the 1970s also ardently supported green revolution technology. The various coalition governments pushed intensive cash-cropping and fostered what they hoped would be increased production through heavy reliance on inputs associated with the green revolution. By the 1990s, Kerala had the third-highest use of chemical inputs tied to green revolution crops among Indian states, a ranking that eerily reflected their standing in farmer suicides a decade later. Despite the amount of land shifted to other crops, governments sought in vain to keep up rice production, increasing chemical inputs and concentrating production on a very limited number of varieties, rather than the multitude of different varieties geared to localized conditions that had been used previously.

Small producers often shifted out of rice production to more lucrative crops, but there were concerns about these crops as well. For much of this time, the most profitable such crop was rubber. Rubber is especially hard on land over time. Other favoured perennial crops included coffee, pepper, tea, and the traditional favourite, coconuts. Producers of all of these were soon caught in a spiral of rapidly declining income, increased costs and falling yields.

Many of the perennial crops small farmers adopted to increase income required significant capital investment. Some farmers also became dependent on expensive chemical inputs and still suffered from falling yields.

This was especially true for pepper and coffee crops, both of which suffered from significant problems by the late 1990s. Pepper developed a widespread fungal disease that devastated crops. Kerala's coffee, a variety of Robusto or a hybrid from Arabica, also suffered. Fungal disease and coffee rust are widespread, and the international price of coffee declined dramatically in the years immediately after its production increased in Kerala. Other small farmer cash crops also declined in value. Rubber prices tumbled in the 1980s. Even coconuts, the mainstay of Kerala small farmers, were no longer a safe bet. The government stopped purchasing them at a guaranteed price, and shortly after, the demand and price for them fell, partly because coconut oil was replaced by palm oil for certain uses.[40] The focus on cash crops and chemical inputs meant that multicropping, traditionally used in very small holdings, which allowed for the cultivation of foodstuffs along with some cash crops, was no longer viable. Many small farmers rely on informal moneylenders and the interest rate for loans to small farmers rarely falls below 8 percent. With declining yields, falling prices, growing devastation of land and water sources and steadily rising costs, Kerala's small farmers were caught in an ever-tightening vice.[41]

Small farmers all over Kerala felt this pressure. However, it was most extreme in the eastern hill regions where farmers had most fully embraced perennial cash crops. By the 1970s, Wayanad, a region described as being completely turned over to coffee, pepper and tea crops, was also the one with the deepest stress and the highest rate of suicide. Small coffee producers were particularly devastated, many simply cutting down the trees they had nurtured for many years. Others were forced to let the trees whither without the inputs on which they depended, harvesting what they could from the devastated crops.[42]

There were widespread and increasing concerns about the costs of the green revolution in India generally and in Kerala specifically. As early as 1985, the Second Citizens' Report on India: The State of the Environment likened the green revolution to the effects of British colonialism and warned about "relentless degradation and destruction." Through to the early 2000s, there were increasing warnings from scientific and government sources about the effects of this form of agriculture on the environment and people's health. Some widely publicized poisonings from the use of Endosulfan, coupled with reports about environmental problems along Kerala's important coastline, prompted calls for action.

Despite these problems, some scientists and politicians continued to support the combined focus on cash crops and green revolution technology. In 1972, Indira Gandhi dismissed arguments about the environmental costs of the green revolution, declaring at the United Nations that if pollution is the price of progress, her people wanted more of it. Closer to home, in the early 2000s, a coalition of scientists and officials working in the agricultural extension office in Kerala, perhaps concerned about their jobs, argued that despite problems, the green revolution had saved millions of lives. They called for a further focus on science and inputs in what they termed the "evergreen revolution." They swore that warnings about the environment accompanied by calls for a different type of agriculture were tied to such nefarious movements as ecofeminism, deep ecology and eco-fascism.[43]

Nevertheless, by the beginning of the new millennium, it was clear change was needed, and the Left Democratic Front in Kerala began widespread consultations on a new era in Kerala agriculture. We can envision how that might look if we explore more fully the potential strengths of small-scale agriculture in Kerala, and in the process, answer some of the critics of Kerala's peasant agriculture.

Hutdweller Gardens

As we have seen, many of the critics of Kerala's agrarian reform argued that it provided land to too many people in too-small parcels. Dismissing arguments, including those from some well-known economists, that mechanization in locations with available labour was counter-productive, these critics have argued that this small size has led to a failure to mechanize and the stunted development of agriculture. Others have suggested, with little evidence, that smallholdings are not productive or efficient, or even that only those with non-farm incomes were able to benefit from the land received through agrarian reform.[44]

Careful exploration of these arguments and what actually goes on in multicropped smallholdings in Kerala leads to a different assessment. A study for the Kerala Institute for Development in 2000 found no evidence of a relationship between non-farm income and the productivity of holdings. It stressed that on marginal and small landholdings, owners "make intense use of their land and cultivate a variety of crops .... most crops are cultivated under a multi-tier cropping system in and around the homesteads. In most homesteads, coconut is the base crop[;] pepper, plantain, arecanut, and tapioca are grown as inter-crops." This contrasted with the pattern in large landholdings, where monocropping of tea, coffee and rubber or rice was most common.[45]

Indeed, this description of multicropping on smallholdings might not have captured fully the complexity and efficiency of such small-scale agriculture in Kerala. Careful assessments of such agriculture provide descriptions that are reminiscent of house gardens in Jamaica or *milpa* agriculture in Central America described earlier. One description for an article in the *Food and Nutrition Bulletin* in 1995 provided this account:

> The spaces between coconut plants are used to raise an array of intercrops, resulting in a multi-storey cropping pattern with distinct canopy stratification. Thus, perennial crops such as coconut, areca nut, jack, mango, cashew, tamarind, and forest tree species occupy the upper layer; pepper, clove, nutmeg, cinnamon, and so on occupy the second layer; banana, cassava, yam and the like occupy the third layer; and ginger, turmeric, pineapple, vegetables, and guinea grass occupy the ground layer. The resultant canopy architecture often approaches that of a tropical rain forest in its structure and species diversity.[46]

The authors found that such complexity is a deliberate attempt to harness as much solar energy as possible and to maintain soil fertility and moisture levels through careful and painstaking cultivation. Food and household demands are met while leaving room for some cash crops. Plants have diverse uses, from foodstuffs to medicine, construction material, green manure and privacy. Of course, such cultivation is not possible using high levels of chemical inputs and this complexity resists mechanization. But rather than leading to stunted agricultural development, this might in fact be a salvation for those small farmers caught in a cycle of spiralling debt.

There are constraints to such a solution. Like intensive agriculture we have examined in multiple other locations around the world, hutdwellers' house gardens are remarkably productive — but such productivity has its limits and requires significant labour expenditure. The limits are mostly a function of access to land. Despite agrarian reform, the poorest 60 percent of the population in Kerala controls less than 2 percent of the cultivated land, and by 2011–12, the average amount of land available in rural landholdings had declined to 0.17 of a hectare. The diminished size of landholdings was partly a function of population increase, but it was mostly the result of the agrarian reforms' failure to implement effectively the cap on land outlined in the 1969 Land Reform Amendment Act. The share of cultivated land controlled by the richest 20 percent of the population increased from just under 74 percent to almost 88 percent between 1983 and 2011–12.[47]

Even with the surprising productivity of carefully maintained house gardens, maintaining such tiny plots of land is often not the most attractive use of hutdwellers' labour. With returns limited and the costs of chemical inputs rising, many rural-dwellers are forced to find work elsewhere, often not locally. The complexity and abundance of both house gardens and the accompanying permaculture suffer as the necessary labour cannot be devoted to the land. The rural poor turn to simpler types of cultivation and permaculture, often geared to the highest return for the least amount of labour. The result is a vicious cycle of declining complexity, yield and environmental health of house gardens and permaculture plots that heightens the need for labour to find outlet elsewhere.[48]

In early 2000, the Left Democratic Front government began a long consultation with citizens focused on the combined crises of agriculture and the environment. The result of those negotiations was the declaration by the government that Kerala as a state would transition to fully organic production over the next two decades.[49] The state government has adopted this approach partly as a branding strategy to foster increased markets for some export crops grown on large plantations. A significant amount of the push for this change, though, came from localized initiatives focused on reviving small-scale agriculture and house garden production. One local project using 100 acres converted to organic rice cultivation, mixed with various other diverse crops, produced rice and excess for the markets for sixty-six families as well as a further 9,130 kilos of organic vegetables, over a quarter of which were marketed.[50] Indeed, numerous commentators have argued that the push for revived small-scale agriculture, embracing the organic nature of traditional agroecology in multicropped smallholdings, is driven primarily by dynamic popular organizations, a function of Kerala's long history of popular activism.[51] Perhaps a return to the future *is* possible.

NOTES

1   Sulfas, an Endosulfan, was banned in India in 2005. Furadan is a carbamate and is widely used throughout India though banned in Canada, the EU, and effectively, the United States. In 2011, the Left Democratic Front in Kerala banned eleven commonly used pesticides. See Toby Bonvoisin, Leah Utyasheva, Duleeka Kniep, David Gunnell and Michael Eddleston, "Suicide by Pesticide Poisoning in India," *BMC Public Health* 20 (2020), 251 <https://doi.org/10.1186/s12889-020-8339-z>.

2   Richard Franke and Barbara Chasin, *Kerala: Radical Reform as Development in an Indian State,* Oakland: Food First, 1994, xi.

3   Kerala had the third highest rate of farmer suicides among all states in India in 2006. Government of India, National Crime Records Bureau of India, 2006, cited in Sapna Thottathil, "!ncredible Kerala?" PhD Dissertation, UC Berkeley, 2012, 16.

4   Stanley Wolpert, *A New History of India*, Oxford: Oxford University Press, 2008; Ranajit Guha, *Dominance without Hegemony: History and Power in Colonial India*, Harvard: Harvard University Press, 1998.

5   Patrick Heller, *The Labor of Development: Workers and the Transformation of Capitalism in Kerala, India*, Ithaca: Cornell University Press, 2000, 59–63; Manali Desai, "Indirect British Rule, State Formation and Welfarism in Kerala, India, 1860–1957," *Social Science History* 29:3 (2005), 457–488.

6   Heller, *The Labor of Development*, 2000, 67; Md Amid Husain and Firoj High Sirwar, "A Comparative Study of Zamindari, Raiyatwari and Mahalwari Land Revenue Settlements: The Colonial Mechanisms of Surplus Extraction in 19th Century British India," *International Journal of Humanities and Social Sciences* 2:4 (2012), 16–26; Thomas Metcalf, *Ideologies of the Raj: The New Cambridge History of India, Vol. 4*, Cambridge: Cambridge University Press, 1994, esp. 25–36.

7   T.C. Varghese, *Agrarian Change and Economic Consequences: Land Tenures in Kerala, 1850–1960*, Bombay: Allied Publishers, 1970.

8   Franke and Chasin, *Kerala*, 1994, 56–57.

9   Stephen Frederic Dale, *Islamic Society on the South Asian Frontier: The Māppilas of Malabar, 1498–1922*, Oxford: Clarendon Press, 1980; Simon James Bytheway, "The Moplah Rebellion Reconsidered: Islamic Insurrection in Southern India, 1921–1922," *Journal of International Studies* 6, (2020), 37–66; P. Radhakrishnan, *Peasant Struggles, Land Reforms and Social Change: Malabar 1836–1982*, New Delhi: Sage Publications, 1989.

10 Philip, *Civilizing Natures*, 2004, 49–51; Ranjit R.J. Daniels and Jayshree Venatesan, *Western Ghats: Biodiversity, People, Conservation*, New Delhi: Rupa &Co., 2008.

11 K.C. John, *Kerala — The Melting Pot*, New Delhi; Nunes Publishers, 1991, 48–66.

12 Ronald Herring, "Contesting the 'Great Transformation': Local Struggles with the Market in South India," in James C. Scott and Nina Bhatt (eds.), *Agrarian Studies: Synthetic Work at the Cutting Edge*, New Haven: Yale University Press, 2001, 235–263, esp. 239.

13 P. Radhakrishnan, "Land Reforms in Theory and Practice: The Kerala Experience," *Economic and Political Weekly* 16: 52 (1981), 129–135; P. Radhakrishnan, "Land Reforms and Changes in Land Systems: Study of a Kerala Village," *Economic and Political Weekly* 17:39 (1982), 107–111; R.W. Franke, "Land Reform versus Inequality in Nadur Village, Kerala," *Journal of Anthropological Research* 48:2 (1992), 81–116.

14 A.V. Jose, "Agrarian Reforms in Kerala — The Role of Peasant Organizations," *Journal of Contemporary Asia* 14:1 (1984), 48–61; Ollie Tornquist, "The New Popular Politics of Development: Kerala's Experience," in Govindan Parayil (ed.), *Kerala: The Development Experience. Reflections on Sustainability and Replicability*, London: Zed Press, 2000, 116–138.

15 K. Mahadevan and M. Sumangala, *Social Development, Cultural Change, and Fertility Decline: A Study of Fertility Change in Kerala*, New Delhi: Sage, 1987.

16 Census of India, 2001; also see Amartya Sen, *Development as Freedom*, New York: Anchor Books, 1999, 189–203; K.P. Kannan, "Poverty Alleviation as Advancing Basic Human Capabilities: Kerala's Achievements Compared," in Parayil (ed.),

Kerala, 2000, 40–65.

17   Govindan Parayil, "Introduction," 1–15, in Parayil (ed.), *Kerala* 2000, esp. 4.

18   Heller, *The Labor of Development,* 2000, 6–7; Franke and Chasin, *Kerala,* 1994, xxi.

19   Bill Mckibben, "The Enigma of Kerala," 1995. *Utne Reader* online newsletter (https://www.utne.com/community/theenigmaofkerala/).

20   T.G. Jacob, *Wayanad: Misery in an Emerald Bowl,* Mumbai: Vikas Adhiyayan Kendra, 2006, 115–116.

21   Joseph Tharamangalam, "The Perils of Social Development without Economic Growth: The Development Debacle in Kerala, India," *Bulletin of Concerned Asian Scholars* 30:1 (1998), 23–34, esp. 24, 27; K. Ravi Raman, "The Kerala Model: Situating the Critique," in K. Ravi Raman (ed.), *Development, Democracy and the State,* London: Routledge, 2010; K.K. George, "Historical Roots of the Kerala Model and Its Present Crisis," *Bulletin of Concerned Asian Scholars* 30:4 (1998), 35–40.

22   Pulapre Balakrishnan, "Land Reforms and the Question of Food in Kerala," *Economic and Political Weekly,* 34:21 (1999), 1272–1280, esp. 1277; C.R. Yadu, "Some Aspects of Agrarian Change in Kerala," *Journal of Land and Rural Studies* 5, 1 (January 2017), 12–30, esp. 15–16.

23   R. Mahesh, "Farm-Size Productivity Relationship: Some Evidence from Kerala," Kerala Institute for Environment and Development, Working Paper #2, 2000, 9.

24   Heller, *The Labor of Development,* 2000, 118.

25   N. Karunakaran, "Paddy Cultivation in Kerala — Trends, Determinants and Effects on Food Security," *Artha Journal of Social Sciences* 13:4 (2014), 21–35, esp. 22; Jeemol Unni, "Changes in the Cropping Pattern in Kerala: Some Evidence on Substitution of Coconut for Rice, 1960–61 to 1978–79," *Economic and Political Weekly* 18:39 (1983),100–107.

26   Karunakaran, "Paddy Cultivation," 2014; Heller, *The Labor of Development,* 2000, 124; Thomas A. Fox, Jeanine M. Rhemtulla, Navin Ramankutty, Corey Lesk, Theraesa Coyle, and T.K Kunhamu, "Agricultural Land-Use Change in Kerala, India: Perspectives from Above and Below the Canopy," *Agriculture, Ecosystems and Environment* 245 (2017), 1–10.

27   Balakrishnan, "Land Reforms," 1999, 1278.

28   K.P. Kannan and A. Pushpangadan, "Agricultural Stagnation in Kerala: An Exploratory Analysis," *Economic and Political Weekly* 23:39 (1988), 120–128.

29   R. Mahesh, "Farm Size Productivity Relationship," 2000, 8.

30   Tharamangalam, "The Perils of Social Development," 1998, 28. See also A. Chakkraborthy, "Kerala's Changing Development Narratives," *Economic and Political Weekly* 40:6 (2005), 541–547 for a discussion of Kerala's increasing pace of economic growth in the 1990s.

31   Radhakrishnan, "Land Reforms in Theory and Practice," 1981, 129–135; see also M.A. Oommen, *Essays on Kerala Economy,* New Delhi: Oxford, 1993.

32   Yadu, "Some Aspects," 2017, 20–21; see also R.K. Raman, "Breaking New Ground: Adivasi Land Struggle in Kerala," *Economic and Political Weekly* 37:10 (2002).

33   Suma Scaria, "Changes in Land Relations: The Political Economy of Land

Reforms in a Kerala Village," *Economic and Political Weekly* 45; 26.27 (2010), 191–198; M.B. Morrison, "The Embourgeoisement of the Kerala Farmer," *Modern Asian Studies* 31:1 (1997), 61–87.

34 John Friedmann, *Empowerment: The Politics of Alternative Development*, Hoboken, NJ: Wiley-Blackwell, 1992.

35 The quote comes from the 1803 edition of *An Essay on the Principle of Population*, Vol. II, 127–128. Malthus's focus on increasing needs as a spur to economic growth was most apparent in his 1820 publication, *Principles of Political Economy*, esp. 470–471. For further discussion see Handy, *Apostles of Inequality*, 2022.

36 Nick Cullather, *The Hungry World: America's Cold War Battle Against Poverty in Asia*, Cambridge, MA: Harvard University Press, 2010; T.C. Olsson, *Agrarian Crossings: Reformers and the Remaking of the US and Mexican Countryside*, Princeton, NJ: Princeton University Press, 2017; John Perkins, *Geopolitics and the Green Revolution: Wheat, Genes, and the Cold War*, Oxford: Oxford University Press, 1997; Eric Ross, "Malthusianism, Capitalist Agriculture, and the Fate of Peasants in the Making of the Modern World Food System," *Review of Radical Political Economics*, 35:4 (2003), 437–461.

37 B.R. Siegel, *Hungry Nation: Food, Famine, and the Making of Modern India*, Cambridge: Cambridge University Press, 2018; Raj Patel, "The Long Green Revolution," *The Journal of Peasant Studies* 40 (2013), 243–263.

38 K. Subramanian, "Revisiting the Green Revolution: Irrigation and Food Production in 20th Century India," PhD dissertation, Kings College London, 2015, 45.

39 For example, the index of input prices for rice production in Andra Pradesh and West Bengal multiplied by six between 1971 and 1989–1990. T. Haque, *Sustainability of Small Holder Agriculture in India*, New Delhi: Concept Publishing Company, 1996, 31–35; see also David Pimental and Marcia Pimentel, "Comment: Adverse Environmental Consequences of the Green Revolution," *Population and Development Review* 16 Supplement (1990), 329–332.

40 Terah Sportel and René Véron problematize this argument somewhat in "Coconut Crisis in Kerala? Mainstream Narrative and Alternative Perspectives," *Development and Change* 47:5 (2016), 1051–1077. See fuller discussion in Note 48 below.

41 P.D. Jeromi "Farmers' Indebtedness and Suicides: Impact of Agricultural Trade Liberalisation in Kerala," *Economic and Political Weekly* 42:31 (2007); Jacob, *Wayanad*, 2006, 7, 89.

42 Thottathil, "!ncredible Kerala," 2012, 47–49; Jacob, *Wayanad*, 2006, 14; Jose George and P. Krishnaprasad, "Agrarian Distress and Farmers' Suicides in the Tribal District of Wayanad," *Social Scientist* 34:7/8 (2006), 70–85.

43 See also P. I. Devi, "Pesticides in Agriculture — a Boon or a Curse? A Case Study of Kerala," *Economic and Political Weekly* 45:26/27 (2010), 199–207.

44 Scaria, "Changes in Land Relations," 2010, 197.

45 Mahesh, "Farm Size Productivity," 2000, 9–11.

46 M. Abdul Salam, K. Sathees Babu and N. Mohanakumaran, "Nutrition and Agriculture: Home Garden Agriculture in Kerala Revisited," *Food and Nutrition Bulletin* 16:3 (1995), 1–15, esp. 1–2.

47 Yadu, "Some Aspects," 2017, 16.
48 Fox et al., "Agricultural Land Use Change," 2017, esp. 6–7; Terah Sportel and René Véron report that this constraint contributed to increased coconut production in south Kerala despite falling prices, as coconuts were much less labour-intensive than a typical mixed permaculture plot. See Sportel and Veron, "Coconut Crisis in Kerala?" (2016), 1069.
49 Government of Kerala, Kerala's State Organic Farming and Strategy Action Plan, Thiruvananthapuram: The Kerala State Biodiversity Board, 2010.
50 Thottathil, "!ncredible Kerala," 2012, 71.
51 Antony Palackal, "Organic Agriculture in Kerala: A Counter-discourse from the Margins," *Sociological Bulletin*, 68:2 (2019), 169–182, esp. 180.

Conclusion: "A Sweet Habit of the Blood"

In his collection of stories set in a small village in the French Alps, John Berger argues that peasants stood on the frontier of society, a position that made their livelihoods more durable but also made it easier for others to justify taking "surplus" from them. As Berger says, their dreams are of "an unhandicapped life, a life in which he is not first forced to produce a surplus before feeding himself." For Berger, peasants are survivors, above all else: "the only characteristic fully shared by peasants everywhere." But despite their many centuries of survival and despite "ideals ... located in the past," Berger argues their "obligations are to the future." In fact, he suggests, peasants are always living in the future: they live in anticipation of the harvest, of the coming rains, of calves and kids and children to come, but also of future "ambushes."[1] Berger's discussion captures well what I hoped to portray about peasant livelihoods and the multiple afflictions they have endured. His balancing of the importance of the past and the future in peasant visions of the world does likewise.

This book was meant to be a discussion of the history of peasant productivity and the various persecutions — ambushes — they have endured. It portrays, I hope convincingly, the extraordinary efficiency with which peasants — English cottagers, Jamaican ex-slaves, Guatemalan Mayan campesinos, Nigerian hill farmers and Kerala hutdwellers — have drawn often bountiful harvests from small bits of land, most often sufficient to feed themselves and their families and to market the surplus. It draws those descriptions very often from commentators who were initially unsympathetic to such livelihoods. Time after time, observers were amazed — sometimes delighted and sometimes dismayed — at the way intensive labour on intercropped plots of land — carefully worked in ways both informed by experience and open to prudent experimentation — could produce such bounty, year after year, generation after generation.

This book also attempts to portray the various ways these livelihoods have been obstructed and attacked, and the arguments used to justify those attacks. It shows that though the protagonists have changed, the arguments remain remarkably consistent. Peasants were ambushed because they were reluctant to provide labour to capitalists, because they were thought prone to having too many children, because they threatened the environment, and because their limited needs meant they could never contribute decisively to economies built on incessant expansion and accumulation.

While a work of history, this book is not primarily directed at the past. Or perhaps, like Berger's peasants, it was located in the past but maintains a vision of the future — as do all explorations of the past. As Lewis Namier (Wola Okrzejska) said many decades ago, historians "remember the future and imagine the past."[2] The future this book remembers is one in which we have learned enough from the past to lose the false confidence that we can know the dreams of others, that we can assume we know what they most desire, that science and sophistication provide answers for questions we cannot imagine, and that we can better others' lives by ignoring those unanticipated questions. This future asks us to be humble, to be ready to learn from apparently simple but in fact extraordinarily complex lives.

Let us return, for a moment, to Robert Andjelic's dreams of an agrarian empire in Saskatchewan. I have no idea at this moment what the response has been to his offer of 22,000 acres of land for rent, so improved that no natural feature of the landscape would inhibit farming the land "from corner to corner." But as I write this, farmers all around me are watching crops wither in the fields and are chopping up a mostly useless harvest for low-grade animal feed as the prairies, and much of the rest of North America, endure a long drought and the hottest weather in recorded history. We can pretend, as Andjelic would surely like us to, that the two are not related, that our experiment with industrial agriculture over the last two centuries is somehow sustainable, necessary to feed the world and does not contribute to global warming.

Instead, this history of peasant productivity and the ambushes they have endured suggests that a more clearly imagined future should include determined measures to assist peasant livelihoods: providing sufficient land, supporting peasant marketing arrangements, assisting in the provision of defensible life spaces and building suitable transportation infrastructure. Above all, such an image of the future should prompt governments, development agencies and specialists to get out of their way, to themselves stop ambushing peasants. Getting out of the way would do more to build sustainable futures and decent lives than a hundred dams or a thousand agricultural modernization projects. Doing so would also begin to embrace the concept of food sovereignty that peasants around the world have been demanding for decades through the Vía Campesina.[3]

At the beginning of the 19th century, Arthur Young — newly concerned about the condition of the rural poor and questioning the wisdom and justice of the agricultural revolution he had so ardently championed — and Thomas Robert Malthus engaged in a very public dispute. Young was better known and much more respected as a commentator on agriculture and conditions in the countryside, although his stock among the rich and powerful was rapidly declining as he took up the cause of the poor. Malthus was just beginning his rapid ascent among the ranks of political economists, one driven primarily by the fact that he provided "advice to the poor for the rich to read" as the poet Robert Southey suggested.[4] His standing was dependent largely on the 1803 expanded and revised edition of the *Principle of Population*. Both Young and Malthus argued they were most concerned with finding ways to reduce the terrible poverty that had descended on a large portion of the rural inhabitants of England. Young pressed hard for sufficient land to be given to cottagers to raise a family in some comfort. Malthus blamed the poor for their own poverty, counselled the end of poor relief and opposed providing the rural poor with land. Young argued he would address that poverty by providing the poor with what they most desired: a small piece of land to farm and, perhaps, raise a pig or two, and a cottage to nurture a family in a community of peers. Malthus asserted he would address that poverty precisely by denying the poor what they most ardently wished for and instead allow their labour to be commanded by capital for the benefit, he said, of all.[5]

It seems to me that basic argument has continued in the centuries since. Peasants, from their marginal position on the frontier of society, have consistently asserted that they want most to survive but to do so with fewer ambushes, perhaps a bit more land and greater control over what they produce and how they produce it. Those pushing progress or improvement or development assured them and others that they knew better and followed policies that made peasant livelihoods much more precarious. Perhaps it is time to return to that argument and position ourselves decisively on the side of Arthur Young.

NOTES

The phrase used in the title of this chapter, "a sweet habit of the blood," comes from a quote in George Eliot's (Mary Ann Evan's) *Daniel Deronda*, first published in 1876. Eliot was not referring specifically to peasants here but was talking about being rooted in the land and sharing work with neighbours, which captures well some of the ideas discussed here. I also like the phrase.

1   John Berger, *Pig Earth*, New York: Pantheon Books, 1979, 196–205.

2   Lewis Namier, "Symmetry and Repetition," in *Conflicts* [1942], reprinted in *Oxford Book of Essays*, Oxford: Oxford University Press, 1991, 432; J.H. Plumb repeated this assertion in *The Death of the Past*, London: Macmillan, 1969.

3   See Annette Aurélie Desmarais, *La Vía Campesina: Globalization and the Power of Peasants*, Winnipeg: Fernwood Publishing, 2007; Hannah Wittman, Annette Aurélie Desmarais and Nettie Wiebe (eds.), *Food Sovereignty: Reconnecting Food, Nature and Community*, Winnipeg: Fernwood Publishing, 2010.

4   Cited in Patricia James, *Population Malthus: His Life and Times*, London: Routledge, 1979, 114–115.

5   This dispute was played out in various publications from both authors: see Arthur Young, "On the Application of the Principle of Population to the Question of Assigning Land to Cottages," *Annals of Agriculture* 41 (1804), 208–231, esp. 213, 226–227, 219–220; and Malthus, *An Essay on the Principle of Population*, 1989 [1803] and the appendix to the 1806 edition of *Principle*.

Bibliography

Abdul Salam, M., K. Sathees Babu and N. Mohanakumaran. 1995. "Nutrition and Agriculture: Home Garden Agriculture in Kerala Revisited." *Food and Nutrition Bulletin* 16, 3: 1.

Allen, Robert. 2008 "The Nitrogen Hypothesis and the English Agricultural Revolution: A Biological Analysis." *Journal of Economic History* 68:182–210.

Altieri, Miguel, et al. 1987. *Agroecology: The Science of Sustainable Agriculture.* Boulder: Westview Press.

Armstrong, Alan, and J.P. Huzel. 1985. "Labour II: Food, Shelter, and Self-Help, the Poor Law and the Position of the Labourer in Rural Society." In G.E. Mingay (ed.), *The Agrarian History of England and Wales Vol. VI.* Cambridge: Cambridge University Press: 729–835.

Balakrishnan, Pulapre. 1999. "Land Reforms and the Question of Food in Kerala." *Economic and Political Weekly* 34, 21: 1272–1280.

Barclay, Alexander. 1827. *A Practical View of the Present State of Slavery in the West Indies,* 2nd ed. London: Smith, Elder & Co.

Barillas, Edgar. 1988. "El problema del Indio durante la Epoca Liberal." Unpublished manuscript.

Barringer, Tim. 2018. "Land, Labor, Landscape: Views of the Plantation in Victorian Jamaica." In Tim Barringer and Wayne Modest (eds.), *Victorian Jamaica.* Durham: Duke University Press: 281–321.

Beckford, William. 1790. *A Descriptive Account of the Island of Jamaica* (2 vols.). London: T. and J. Egerton.

Benke. Roy H., and Michael Mortimore (eds.). 2016. *The End of Desertification? Disputing Environmental Change in the Drylands.* Berlin: Springer-Verlag.

Berger, John. 1979. *Pig Earth.* New York: Pantheon Books.

Bergius, Mikael, and Jill Tove Buseth. 2019. "Towards a Green Modernization Development Discourse: the New Green Revolution in Africa." *Journal of Political Ecology* 26: 57–83.

Bernard, Sir Thomas. 1798. "An Account of a Cottage and Garden." *Annals of Agriculture, and Other Useful Arts* 30: 149–151.

Besson, Jean. 2002. *Martha Brae's Two Histories: European Expansion and Caribbean Culture-Building in Jamaica.* Chapel Hill: University of North Carolina Press.

Bigelow, John. 2006 [1851]. *Jamaica in 1850: or, the Effects of Sixteen Years of Freedom on a Slave Colony.* Chicago: University of Illinois Press.

Blackburn, Robin. 1997. *The Making of New World Slavery: from the Baroque to the Modern, 1492–1800.* London: Verso.

Bonvoisin, Toby, Leah Utyasheva, Duleeka Kniep, David Gunnell and Michael Eddleston. 2020. "Suicide by Pesticide Poisoning in India." *BMC Public Health* 20: 251. <https://doi.org/10.1186/s12889-020-8339-z>.

Boserup, Ester. 1990. *Economic and Demographic Relationships in Development* (ed. T. Paul Schultz). Baltimore: Johns Hopkins University Press.

Boys, John. 1800. "Crops and Poor." *Annals of Agriculture, and Other Useful Arts* 36: 368–370.

Braudel, Fernand. 1982. *Civilization and Capitalism: Vol 2: The Wheels of Commerce* (trans. Sian Reynolds). London: Williams, Collins and Sons.

British Parliamentary Papers. 1905. *Poor Law Commissioners' Report, 1834.* London: H.M. Stationary Office.

___. 1842. "Report from the Select Committee on West India Colonies." *House of Commons Papers* 479.

___. 1836. "Report from the Select Committee on Negro Apprenticeship in the Colonies." *House of Commons Papers* 560.

___. 1831–1832. "Report of the Select Committee on the Commercial State of the West India Colonies." *House of Commons Papers* 381.

___. 1831–1832. "Report of the Select Committee on the Extinction of Slavery throughout the British Dominions." *House of Commons Papers* 721.

Bunzel, Ruth Leal. 1959. *Chichicastenango: A Guatemalan Village.* Seattle: University of Chicago Press.

Burkitt, R. 1930. "Explorations in the Highlands of Western Guatemala." *The Museum Journal of the University of Pennsylvania* 21.

Burnard, Trevor. 2004. *Mastery, Tyranny, and Desire: Thomas Thistlewood and His Slaves in the Anglo-Jamaican World.* Chapel Hill: University of North Carolina Press.

Butler, Kathleen Mary. 1995. *The Economics of Emancipation, 1823–1843.* Chapel Hill: University of North Carolina Press.

Bytheway, Simon James. 2020. "The Moplah Rebellion Reconsidered: Islamic Insurrection in Southern India, 1921–1922." *Journal of International Studies* 6: 37–66.

Cambranes, J.C. 1985. *Café y campesinos en Guatemala, 1853–1897.* Guatemala: Editorial Universitaria de Guatemala.

___. 1975. *Aspectos del desarrollo económico y social de Guatemala a la luz de fuentes históricas alemanas, 1868–1885.* Guatemala City: Universidad de San Carlos.

Carey, David. 2019. "The Heart of the Country: The Primacy of Peasants and Maize in Modern Guatemala." *Journal of Latin American Studies* 51, 2: 273–306.

Carlyle, Thomas. 1853. *Occasional Discourse on the Nigger Question.* London: Thomas Bosworth. <https://www.americanantiquarian.org/Manuscripts/carlyle.html>.

___. 1843. *Past and Present.* London: Chapman and Hall.

Carmack, Robert. 1995. *Rebels of Highland Guatemala: The Quiché-Mayas of Momostenango.* Norman: University of Oklahoma Press.

_____. 1983. "Spanish-Indian Relations in Highland Guatemala 1800–1944." In Murdo MacLeod and Robert Wasserstrom (eds.), *Spaniards and Indians in Southeastern Mesoamerica*. Lincoln: University of Nebraska Press: 215–253.

_____. 1979. *Historia Social de los Quichés*. Guatemala: José de Pineda Ibarra.

Chakkraborthy, A. 2005. "Kerala's Changing Development Narratives." *Economic and Political Weekly* 40, 6: 541–547.

Chassé, Patrick. 2017. "Produce More to Live Better: Cotton, Corn, and Agrarian Modernization in Guatemala, 1944–1966." PhD dissertation, University of Saskatchewan.

Checkland, S.G. and E.O.A. Checkland (eds.). 1974. *The Poor Law Report of 1834*. Harmondshire: Penguin.

Cleave, John. 1974. *African Farmers: Labor Use in the Development of Smallholder Agriculture*. New York: Praeger Publishers.

Cobbett, William. 1962. *The Autobiography of William Cobbett* (ed. William Reitzell). London: Faber and Faber Ltd.

_____. 1830. *Rural Rides in the Counties of Surrey, Kent, Hampshire, etc*. London.

_____. 1823. *Cottage Economy*. London.

Cullather, Nick. 2010. *The Hungry World: America's Cold War Battle Against Poverty in Asia*. Cambridge, MA: Harvard University Press.

Curtin, Philip. 1968. *Two Jamaicas: The Role of Ideas in a Tropical Colony, 1830–1865*. New York: Greenwood Press.

Dale, Stephen Frederic. 1980. *Islamic Society on the South Asian Frontier: The Māppilas of Malabar, 1498–1922*. Oxford: Clarendon Press.

Daniels, Ranjit R.J., and Jayshree Venatesan. 2008. *Western Ghats: Biodiversity, People, Conservation*. New Delhi: Rupa & Co.

Daño, Elenita C. 2008. "Unmasking the Green Revolution in Africa." *Rural 21*: 32–36.

Davies, David. 1795. *The Case of Labourers in Husbandry Stated and Considered*. London: G.G. and J. Richardson.

Davis, Sheldon, and Julie Hodson. 1982. *Witnesses to Political Violence in Guatemala: The Suppression of a Rural Development Movement*. Oxfam America Impact Audit.

Davy, John. 1854. *The West Indies Before and Since Slave Emancipation*. London: W&F.G. Cash.

Desai, Manali. 2005. "Indirect British Rule, State Formation and Welfarism in Kerala, India, 1860–1957." *Social Science History* 29, 3: 457–488.

Desmarais, Annette Aurélie. 2007. *La Vía Campesina: Globalization and the Power of Peasants*. Winnipeg: Fernwood Publishing.

Devi, P. I. 2010. "Pesticides in Agriculture — A Boon or a Curse? A Case Study of Kerala." *Economic and Political Weekly* 45, 26/27: 199–207.

Diao, Xinshen, Derek Headey, and Michael Johnson. 2008. "Toward a Green Revolution in Africa: What Would It Achieve, and What Would It Require?" *Agricultural Economics* 39, supplement: 539–550.

Diouf, Sylviane (ed.). 2003. *Fighting the Slave Trade: West African Strategies*. Athens, Ohio: Ohio University Press.

Duncan, Colin. 1996. *The Centrality of Agriculture*. Montreal: McGill-Queens Press.

Dunn, Richard. 1972. *Sugar and Slaves: The Rise of the Planter Class in the English West*

Indies, 1624–1713. Chapel Hill: University of North Carolina Press.

Economist. 1864. "The Food of the English Labourer." Oct. 18: 1252–1253.

———. 1861. "English Feelings Toward America." Sept. 28: 1065–1067.

———. 1859. "African Cotton and Cotton Manufactures in Relation to the Slave Trade." March 5: 251–253.

———. 1859. "The Deficiency of Labour in the West Indies." July 16: 784–786.

———. 1855. "Scarcity of Labour." Sept. 8: 979–980.

———. 1851. "French Husbandry." Sept. 13: 1012–1013.

———. 1849. "Employment of Labour in Husbandry." May 19: 547.

———. 1849. "Land: A Commodity." June 16: 659.

———. 1848. "Can the Slave Trade Be Suppressed." Sept. 2: 993–995.

———. 1848. "The Productiveness of Large and Small Farms." Nov. 25: 1330–1331.

———. 1846. "Agriculture: Land; Its Uses and Abuses." July 11: 893–894.

———. 1845. "The Slave Trade and Slavery — Mr. Hutt's Motion." June 28: 597–598.

———. 1844. "Provinces." Sept. 28: 1259.

———. 1844. "The Labourer's Panacea — The Allotment System." Nov. 2: 1369–1370.

———. 1843. "Free Trade and Slave Trade." Nov. 4: 156.

———. 1843. "Rebecca Riots." Oct. 14: 105.

———. 1843. "Scientific Agriculture for Farmers." Sept. 9: 27.

Edwards, Bryan. 1806. *The History, Civil and Commercial, of the British Colonies in the West Indies,* 4 Vols. Philadelphia: James Humphreys.

Ehrlich, Paul. 1968. *The Population Bomb: Population Control or Race to Oblivion?* San Francisco: Sierra Club.

Eisner, Gisela. 1961. *Jamaica, 1830–1930: A Study in Economic Growth.* Manchester: Manchester University Press.

Eliot, George. 1876. *Daniel Deronda.* London: William Blackwood and Sons.

Esquit, Edgar. 2013. "Identidades políticas indígenas en la época de la privatización de las tierras en Guatemala, finales del siglo XIX." *Territorios* VIII (Nov.): 75–96.

Fox, Thomas A., Jeanine M. Rhemtulla, Navin Ramankutty, Corey Lesk, Theraesa Coyle, and T.K Kunhamu. 2017. "Agricultural Land-Use Change in Kerala, India: Perspectives from Above and Below the Canopy." *Agriculture, Ecosystems and Environment* 245: 1–10.

Franke, Richard. 1992. "Land Reform versus Inequality in Nadur Village, Kerala." *Journal of Anthropological Research* 48, 2: 81–116.

Franke, Richard, and Barbara Chasin. 1994. *Kerala: Radical Reform as Development in an Indian State,* Oakland: Food First.

Friedmann, John. 1992. *Empowerment: The Politics of Alternative Development.* Hoboken, NJ: Wiley-Blackwell.

Fussell, G.E. 1943. "My Impressions of Arthur Young." *Agricultural History Review* 17: 135–144.

Gallina, Stefania. 2009. *Una historia ambiental del café en Guatemala.* Guatemala: AVANCSO.

García Laguardia, Jorge Mario. 1977. *El pensamiento liberal de Guatemala.* San José, Costa Rica: Educa.

Gazley, John G. 1973. *The Life of Arthur Young.* Philadelphia: American Philosophical Society.

George, Jose, and P. Krishnaprasad. 2006. "Agrarian Distress and Farmers' Suicides in the Tribal District of Wayanad." *Social Scientist* 34, 7/8: 70–85.

George, K.K. 1998. "Historical Roots of the Kerala Model and Its Present Crisis." *Bulletin of Concerned Asian Scholars* 30, 4: 35–40.

Gollas-Quintero M. 1969. "History and Economic Theory in the Analysis of the Development of Guatemalan Indian Agriculture." PhD dissertation, University of Wisconsin.

González-Izás, Matilde. 2014. *Modernización capitalista, racismo y violencia: Guatemala, 1750–1930.* Mexico: El Colegio de México.

Goubaud Carrera, Antonio. 1947. "Reconnaissance of Northern Guatemala, 1944." *Manuscript Collections of Middle American Anthropology (MACA)* #17. Chicago: University of Chicago Press.

Grandin, Greg. 2004. *The Last Colonial Massacre: Latin America in the Cold War,* Chicago: University of Chicago Press.

Guatemala, Government of. 2004. *IV Censo Nacional Agropecuario.* Guatemala: Dirección general de estadística.

____. 1979. *III Censo Nacional Agropecuario.* Guatemala: Dirección general de estadística.

____. 1954. *Censo agropecuario, 1950.* Guatemala: Dirección general de estadística.

____. 1953. *Informe del ciudadano presidente de la república, coronel Jacobo Arbenz Guzmán al congreso.* Guatemala: Secretaria de Propaganda y Divulgación de la Presidencia de la República.

____. 1951. Asamblea Constituyente, Guatemala. *Diario de sesiones.* Guatemala City: Tipografía Nacional.

Guatemala, United Nations Mission (MINUGUA). 1999, *Guatemala: Memoria del silencio.* Comisión para el Esclarecimiento Histórico. [*Guatemala*: Memory of Silence, Report of the Commission for the Clarification of History, English language summary].

Guha, Ranajit. 1998. *Dominance without Hegemony: History and Power in Colonial India.* Harvard: Harvard University Press.

Hakewill, James. 1825. *A Picturesque Tour of the Island of Jamaica, from Drawings Made in the Years 1820 and 1821.* London: Hurst and Robinson.

Hall, Catherine. 2002. *Civilising Subjects: Metropole and Colony in the English Imagination, 1830–1867.* Chicago: University of Chicago Press.

Hall, Charles. 1849 [1805]. *The Effects of Civilisation on the People of the European States.* London: John Minter Morgan.

Hall, Douglas. 1959. *Free Jamaica, 1838–1865: An Economic History.* New Haven: Yale University Press.

____. 1989. *In Miserable Slavery: Thomas Thistlewood in Jamaica, 1750–1786.* Basingstoke: MacMillan.

Handy, Jim. 2022. *Apostles of Inequality: Rural Poverty, Political Economy, and the Economist, 1760–1860.* Toronto: University of Toronto Press.

____. 2017. "The Violence of Dispossession: Guatemala in the Nineteenth and Twentieth Centuries." In Sebastian Huhn and Hannes Warnecke-Berger (eds.), *Politics and History of Violence and Crime in Central America.* New York: Palgrave Macmillan.

____. 2009. "'Almost Idiotic Wretchedness': A Long History of Blaming Peasants." *Journal of Peasant Studies* 36, 2: 325–344.

____. 1994. *Revolution in the Countryside.* Chapel Hill: University of North Carolina Press.

____. 1992. "Reforma y Contrareforma: La política agraria en Guatemala, 1952–1957." In Julio Castellanos Cambranes (ed.), *500 Años de lucha por la tierra*, Vol. 1: 379-400. Guatemala City: Facultad Latinoamericana de Ciencias Sociales.

____. 1984. *Gift of the Devil.* Toronto: Between the Lines.

Hane, M. 1982. *Peasants, Rebels, and Outcastes: The Underside of Modern Japan.* New York: Pantheon.

Haque T. 1996. *Sustainability of Small Holder Agriculture in India.* New Delhi: Concept Publishing Company.

Hardin, Garret. 1974. "Living on a Lifeboat." BioScience 24, 10: 561–568.

____. 1968. "The Tragedy of the Commons." *Science* 162, 3859 (Dec.): 1243–1248.

Hart, Keith. 1982. *The Political Economy of West African Agriculture.* Cambridge: Cambridge University Press.

Heller, Patrick. 2000. *The Labor of Development: Workers and the Transformation of Capitalism in Kerala, India.* Ithaca: Cornell University Press.

Herring, Ronald. 2001. "Contesting the 'Great Transformation': Local Struggles with the Market in South India." In James C. Scott and Nina Bhatt (eds.), *Agrarian Studies: Synthetic Work at the Cutting Edge.* New Haven: Yale University Press: 235–263.

Heuman, Gad. 1994. *The Killing Time: The Morant Bay Rebellion in Jamaica.* Knoxville: University of Tennessee Press.

Higbee, E.C. 1947. "The Agricultural Regions of Guatemala." *The Geographical Review* 37: 177–201.

Higman, B.W. 1976. *Slave Population and Economy in Jamaica, 1807–1834* Cambridge: Cambridge University Press.

Hinton, John Howard. 1849. *Memoir of William Knibb, Missionary in Jamaica*, 2nd edition. London: Houlston and Stoneman.

Holt, Thomas C. 1992. *The Problem of Freedom: Race, Labor, and Politics in Jamaica and Britain, 1832–1938.* Baltimore: Johns Hopkins University Press.

Holt-Giménez, Eric. 2008. "Out of AGRA: The Green Revolution Returns to Africa." *Development* 51: 464–471.

Homer-Dixon, Thomas. 1999. *Environment, Scarcity, and Violence.* Princeton: Princeton University Press.

Hopkins, A.G. 1973. *An Economic History of West Africa.* London: Longman.

Husain, Md Amid, and Firoj High Sirwar. 2012. "A Comparative Study of Zamindari, Raiyatwari and Mahalwari Land Revenue Settlements: The Colonial Mechanisms of Surplus Extraction in 19th Century British India." *International Journal of Humanities and Social Sciences* 2, 4: 16–26.

Hyden, Goran. 1980. *Beyond Ujamaa in Tanzania: Underdevelopment and an Uncaptured Peasantry.* Berkeley: University of California Press.

Isakson, Ryan. 2009. "No hay ganancia en la milpa: The Agrarian Question, Food Sovereignty, and the On-Farm Conservation of Agrobiodiversity in the Guatemalan Highlands." *Journal of Peasant Studies* 36, 4: 725–759.

Jacob, T.G. 2006. *Wayanad: Misery in an Emerald Bowl.* Mumbai: Vikas Adhiyayan Kendra.

James, Patricia. 1979. *Population Malthus: His Life and Times.* London: Routledge.

Jeromi. P.D. 2007. "Farmers' Indebtedness and Suicides: Impact of Agricultural Trade Liberalisation in Kerala." *Economic and Political Weekly* 42, 31.

John, K.C. 1991. *Kerala — The Melting Pot.* New Delhi: Nunes Publishers.

Jones, Chester Lloyd. 1940. *Guatemala: Past and Present.* Minneapolis: University of Minnesota Press.

Jones, Peter. 2016. *Agricultural Enlightenment: Knowledge, Technology, and Nature.* Oxford: Oxford University Press.

Jose, A.V. 1984. "Agrarian Reforms in Kerala — The Role of Peasant Organizations." *Journal of Contemporary Asia* 14, 1: 48–61.

Kannan, K.P. 2000. "Poverty Alleviation as Advancing Basic Human Capabilities: Kerala's Achievements Compared." In Govindan Parayil (ed.), *Kerala: The Development Experience.* London: Zed Books: 40–64.

Kannan, K.P., and A. Pushpangadan. 1988. "Agricultural Stagnation in Kerala: An Exploratory Analysis." *Economic and Political Weekly* 23, 39: 120–128.

Kaplan, Robert. 1994. "The Coming Anarchy: How Scarcity, Crime, Overpopulation and Disease are Rapidly Destroying the Social Fabric of our Planet." *The Atlantic,* Feb.: 44–76.

Karunakaran, N. 2014. "Paddy Cultivation in Kerala — Trends, Determinants and Effects on Food Security." *Artha Journal of Social Sciences* 13, 4: 21–35.

Kerala, Government of. 2010 Kerala's State Organic Farming and Strategy Action Plan, Thiruvananthapuram: The Kerala State Biodiversity Board.

Kerr, William. 2011. "Food Sovereignty — Old Protectionism in Somewhat Recycled Bottles." *African Technology and Development Forum Journal* 8: 4–9.

Killen, J. et al. 1995. *The Famine Decade: Contemporary Accounts, 1841–1851.* Belfast: Blackstaff Press.

Koch, Alexander, Chris Brierley, Mark Maslin, and Simon Lewis. 2019. "Earth System Impacts of the European Arrival and Great Dying in the Americas after 1492." *Quaternary Science Reviews* 207: 13–36.

Latouche, Serge. 1993. *In the Wake of the Affluent Society: An Exploration of Post-Development.* London: Zed Books.

Lawrence, Peter. 1988. "The Political Economy of the 'Green Revolution' in Africa." *Review of African Political Economy* 15, 42: 59–75.

Leach, Melissa, and James Fairhead. 1996. *Misreading the African Landscape: Society and Ecology in a Forest-Savanna Mosaic.* Cambridge: Cambridge University Press.

Leach, Melissa, and Robert Mearns (eds.). 1996. *The Lie of the Land: Challenging Received Wisdom on the African Environment.* Oxford: James Currey Ltd.

Lewis, W.A. 1958. "Economic Development with Unlimited Supplies of Labour." In A.N. Agarwala and S.P. Singh (eds.), *The Economics of Underdevelopment.* Oxford: Oxford University Press.

Liebman, Matt. 1987. "Polyculture Cropping Systems." In Miguel Altieri et al, *Agroecology: The Science of Sustainable Agriculture.* Boulder: Westview Press: 205–217.

Lincoln, J. Steward. 1945. "An Ethnological Study of Ixile Indians." MACA #1.

Little-Siebold, Todd. 2001. "'Where Have All the Spaniards Gone': Independent

Identities: Ethnicies, Class and the Emergent National State." *Journal of Latin American and Caribbean Anthropology* 6, 2: 106–133.

Littlewood, Roland. 1985. "Jungle Madness: Some Observations on Expatriate Psychopathology." *International Journal of Social Psychiatry* 9, 31: 3.

Long, Edward. 1774. *The History of Jamaica, General Survey of the Antient and Modern State of that Island: with Reflections on its Situation, Settlements, Inhabitants, Climate, Products, Commerce, Laws, and Government, Vol. II.* London: T. Lowndes, in Fleet-Street.

Lovejoy, Paul. 1981. "Slavery in the Sokoto Caliphate." In Paul Lovejoy (ed.), *The Ideology of Slavery in Africa.* Beverly Hills: Sage Publications: 201–243.

_____. 1978. "Plantations in the Economy of the Sokoto Caliphate." *The Journal of African History* 19, 3: 341–368.

Lovell, George. 1993. "Epidemias y despoblación, 1519–1632." In Jorge Luján Muñoz (ed.), *Historia General de Guatemala*, 2. Guatemala: Fundación para la Cultura y el Desarrollo: 327–36.

_____. 1988. "Surviving Conquest: The Maya of Guatemala in Historical Perspective." *Latin American Research Review* 23, 2: 25–57.

Lovell George, and Christopher Lutz. 1995. *Demography and Empire: A Guide to the Population History of Spanish Central America, 1500–1821.* Boulder: Westview Press.

Madigan, Douglas. 1976. "Santiago Atitlán, Guatemala: A Socioeconomic and Demographic History." PhD dissertation, University of Pittsburgh.

Mahadevan, K., and M. Sumangala. 1987. *Social Development, Cultural Change, and Fertility Decline: A Study of Fertility Change in Kerala.* New Delhi: Sage.

Mahesh, R. 2000. "Farm-Size Productivity Relationship: Some Evidence from Kerala." Kerala Institute for Environment and Development, Working Paper #2.

Malthus, T.R. 1989 [1803]. *An Essay on the Principle of Population, 1803* (ed. Patricia James). Cambridge: Cambridge University Press.

_____. 1989 [1820]. *Principles of Political Economy.* (ed. John Pullen). Cambridge: Cambridge University Press.

Mamdani, Mahmood. 2018. *Citizen and Subject: Contemporary Africa and the Legacy of Late Colonialism.* Princeton: Princeton University Press.

Manz, Beatrice. 2004. *Paradise in Ashes: A Guatemalan Journey of Courage, Terror, and Hope,* . Berkeley: University of California Press.

Marx, Karl. 1967. *Capital Vol. 1.* New York: Progress Publishers.

McCann, James. 1999. *Green Land, Brown Land, Black Land: An Environmental History of Africa, 1800–1990.* Portsmouth, NH: Heinemann.

McCreery, David. 1994. *Rural Guatemala 1760–1940.* Stanford: Stanford University Press.

_____. 1986. "'An Odious Feudalism': *Mandamiento* Labor and Commercial Agriculture in Guatemala, 1858–1920." *Latin American Perspectives* 13, 1: 99–118.

_____. 1983. "Debt Servitude in Rural Guatemala, 1876–1936." *Hispanic American Research Review* 63, 4: 735–739.

McKibben, Bill. "The Enigma of Kerala," 1995. *Utne Reader,* online newsletter (https://www.utne.com/community/theenigmaofkerala/).

McLeod, Murdo. 2008. *Spanish Central America: A Socioeconomic History, 1520–1720,* revised edition. Austin: University of Texas Press. [First published 1973,

Berkeley: University of California Press.]

McLeod, Murdo, and Robert Wasserstrom (eds.). 1983. *Spaniards and Indians in Southeastern Mesoamerica.* Lincoln: University of Nebraska Press.

Meadows, Donella H., et al. 1972. *Limits to Growth.* Washington, DC: Potomac Associates Book.

Metcalf, Thomas. 1994. *Ideologies of the Raj: The New Cambridge History of India, Vol. 4.* Cambridge: Cambridge University Press.

Mill, John Stuart. 1848. *Principles of Political Economy with some of their Applications to Social Philosophy.* London: George Routledge and Sons Ltd.

Mintz, Sidney, and Douglas Hall. 1970. "The Origins of the Jamaican Internal Marketing System." *Yale University Publications in Anthropology* 57.

Mkindi, Abdallah Ramadhani, et al. 2020. *False Promises: The Alliance for a Green Revolution in Africa (AGRA).* Study found in *Grain*: https://grain.org/en/article/6499-false-promises-the-alliance-for-a-green-revolution-in-africa-agra.

Morrison, M.B. 1997. "The Embourgeoisement of the Kerala Farmer." *Modern Asian Studies* 31, 1: 61–87.

Namier, Lewis. 1991. "Symmetry and Repetition." In *Conflicts* [1942] reprint in *Oxford Book of Essays.* Oxford: Oxford University Press.

Náñez Falcón, Guillermo. 1970. "Erwin Paul Dieseldorf, German Entrepreneur in the Alta Verapaz of Guatemala, 1889–1937." PhD dissertation, Tulane.

Netting, Robert McC. 1993. *Smallholders, Householders: Farm Families and the Ecology of Intensive, Sustainable Agriculture.* Stanford: Stanford University Press.

_____. 1968. *Hill Farmers of Nigeria: Cultural Ecology of the Kofyar of the Jos Plateau.* Seattle: University of Washington Press.

Neumann, Roderick. 2002. *Imposing Wilderness: Struggles over Livelihood and Nature Preservation in Africa.* Berkeley: University of California Press.

Oglesby, Elizabeth. 2002. "Politics at Work: Elites, Labor and Agrarian Modernization in Guatemala, 1980–2000." PhD dissertation, University of California, Berkeley.

Oficina de Derechos Humanos del Arzobispado en Guatemala 1998. *Guatemala: Nunca Más.* Proyecto Interdiocesano de Recuperación de la memoria histórico (Remhi), Tomo 1.

Olsson, T.C. 2017. *Agrarian Crossings: Reformers and the Remaking of the US and Mexican Countryside.* Princeton, NJ: Princeton University Press.

Oommen, M.A. 1993. *Essays on Kerala Economy.* New Delhi: Oxford.

Oughton, Samuel. 1862 "The Influence of Artificial Wants on the Social, Moral and Commercial Advancement of Jamaica," *West India Quarterly,* June 1862. Reprinted in *Roupell the Forger, the Lessons of His Crime and Punishment,* 1862. Kingston: DeCordova, McDougall and Co.

Overton, Mark. 1996. *Agricultural Revolution in England: The Transformation of the Agrarian Economy, 1500–1850.* Cambridge: Cambridge University Press.

_____. 1996. "Re-establishing the English Agricultural Revolution." *Agricultural History Review* 44: 1–20.

Palackal, Antony. 2019. "Organic Agriculture in Kerala: A Counter-discourse from the Margins." *Sociological Bulletin* 68, 2: 169–182.

Parayil, Govindan (ed.). 2000. *Kerala: The Development Experience. Reflections on*

Sustainability and Replicability. London: Zed Press.

Patel, Raj. 2013. "The Long Green Revolution." *The Journal of Peasant Studies* 40: 243–63.

Paton, Diana. 2004. *No Bond but the Law: Punishment, Race, and Gender in Jamaican State Formation, 1780–1870*. Durham: Duke University Press.

Perkins, John. 1997. *Geopolitics and the Green Revolution: Wheat, Genes, and the Cold War*. Oxford: Oxford University Press.

Phelps Brown, H., and S.V. Hopkins. 1955. "Seven Centuries of Building Wages." *Economica* 24: 296–314.

Philip, Kavita. 2004. *Civilizing Natures: Race, Resources, and Modernity in Colonial South India*. New Brunswick, NJ: Rutgers.

Phillippo, James M. 1843. *Jamaica: Its Past and Present State*. Philadelphia: James M. Campbell & Co.

Pimentel, David, and Marcia Pimental. 1990. "Comment: Adverse Environmental Consequences of the Green Revolution." *Population and Development Review* 16, Supplement: 329–332.

Plumb, J.H. 1969. *The Death of the Past*. London: Macmillan.

Pulteney, Sir William. 1806. "Accounts of Cottagers." *Annals of Agriculture, and Other Useful Arts* 44: 97–111.

Radhakrishnan, P. 1989. *Peasant Struggles, Land Reforms and Social Change: Malabar 1836–1982*. New Delhi: Sage Publications.

_____. 1982. "Land Reforms and Changes in Land Systems: Study of a Kerala Village." *Economic and Political Weekly* 17, 39: 107–111.

_____. 1981. "Land Reforms in Theory and Practice: The Kerala Experience." *Economic and Political Weekly* 16, 52: 129–135.

Raman, K.R. 2010. "The Kerala Model: Situating the Critique." In K. Ravi Raman (ed.), *Development, Democracy and the State*. London: Routledge.

_____. 2002. "Breaking New Ground: Adivasi Land Struggle in Kerala." *Economic and Political Weekly* 37, 10: 916–919.

Ravenstone, Piercy. 1966 [1821]. *A Few Doubts as to the Correctness of Some Opinions Generally Entertained on the Subjects of Population and Political Economy*. New York: Augustus M. Kelly.

Redfield, Robert. 1980. "April Is This Afternoon: Correspondence of Robert Redfield and Sol Tax, 1933–1944." MACA Series LXIII, University of Chicago Library: 131–307.

Reeves, Rene. 2006. *Ladinos with Ladinos, Indians with Indians: Land, Labor, and Regional Ethnic Conflict in the Making of Guatemala*. Stanford: Stanford University Press.

Richards, Paul. 1985. *Indigenous Agricultural Revolution: Ecology and Food Production in West Africa*. London: Hutchinson.

Rose, Walter. 1964. *Good Neighbours: Some Recollections of an English Village and Its People*. Cambridge: Cambridge University Press.

Ross, Eric. 2003. "Malthusianism, Capitalist Agriculture, and the Fate of Peasants in the Making of the Modern World Food System." *Review of Radical Political Economics* 35, 4: 437–461.

Sánchez, M. Rubio. 1961. "La grana o cochinilla." *Antropología e historia de Guatemala* 3: 15–46.

Sauer, Carl. 2009. *Carl Sauer on Culture and Landscape: Readings and Commentaries.* Baton Rouge: Louisiana State University Press.

Scaria, Suma. 2010. "Changes in Land Relations: The Political Economy of Land Reforms in a Kerala Village." *Economic and Political Weekly* 45, 26.27: 191–198.

Sen, Amartya. 1999. *Development as Freedom.* New York: Anchor Books.

Senior, Nassau. 1947. *Four Introductory Lectures on Political Economy.* London: J. Murray.

____. 1831. *An Introductory Lecture on Political Economy.* London: J. Murray.

Sewell, W.G. 1861. *The Ordeal of Free Labour in the British West Indies.* New York: Harper and Brothers.

Sheller, Mimi. 2000. *Democracy after Slavery: Black Publics and Peasant Radicalism in Haiti and Jamaica.* Gainesville: University Press of Florida.

Sherman, William. 1979. *Forced Native Labor in Sixteenth-Century Central America.* Lincoln: University of Nebraska Press.

Siegel, B.R. 2018. *Hungry Nation: Food, Famine, and the Making of Modern India.* Cambridge: Cambridge University Press.

Sierra, Hector. 1949. "Corn in Guatemala." In I.E. Melhus (ed.), *Plant Research in the Tropics: Research Bulletin 371.* Ames: Iowa State College.

Sinclair, Sir John. 1800. "Observations on the Means of Enabling a Cottager to Keep a Cow by the Produce of a Small Portion of Arable Land." *Annals of Agriculture, and Other Useful Arts* 36: 231–248.

Smith, Adam. 1776. *An Inquiry into the Nature and Causes of the Wealth of Nations.* London: W. Strahan.

Snell, Keith. 2006. *Parish and Belonging: Community, Identity and Welfare in England and Wales, 1700–1950.* Cambridge: Cambridge University Press.

____. 1985. *Annals of the Labouring Poor: Social Change and Agrarian England, 1600–1900.* Cambridge: Cambridge University Press.

Solórzano, V. 1977. *Evolución económica de Guatemala.* Guatemala City: Seminario de integración social.

Sportel, Terah, and René Véron. 2016. "Coconut Crisis in Kerala? Mainstream Narrative and Alternative Perspectives." *Development and Change* 47, 5: 1051–1077.

Stanzione, Vincent. 2003. *Rituals of Sacrifice: Walking the Face of the Earth on the Sacred Path of the Sun.* Albuquerque: University of New Mexico Press.

Sturt, George. 1912. *Change in the Village.* New York: George H. Doran Company.

Subramanian, K. 2015. "Revisiting the Green Revolution: Irrigation and Food Production in 20th Century India." PhD dissertation, Kings College London.

Swift, Jeremy. 1996. "Desertification: Narratives, Winners and Losers." In Leach and Means (eds.), *The Lie of the Land.* Oxford: James Currey.

Taracena Arriola, Arturo. 1997. *Invención criolla, sueño ladino, pesadilla indígena: Los Altos de Guatemala.* San José: Centro de Investigaciones Regionales de Mesoamérica.

Tax, Sol. 1953. *Penny Capitalism.* Washington: US Government Printing Office.

____. 1946. "The Towns of Lake Atitlán." MACA #13 Chicago: University of Chicago.

Tharamangalam, Joseph. 1998. "The Perils of Social Development without Economic Growth: The Development Debacle in Kerala, India." *Bulletin of Concerned Asian*

Scholars 30, 1: 23–34.

Thick, Malcolm. 1985. "Market Gardening in England and Wales." In Thirsk (ed.), *The Agrarian History of England and Wales, Vol. 5: 1640–1750.* Cambridge: Cambridge University Press: 502–532.

Thirsk, Joan. 1985. "Agricultural Innovations and Their Diffusion." In Thirsk (ed.), *The Agrarian History of England and Wales, Vol. 5: 1640–1750.* Cambridge: Cambridge University Press: 533–589.

____. 1985. "Agricultural Policy: Public Debate and Legislation." In Thirsk (ed.), *The Agrarian History of England and Wales, Vol. 5: 1640–1750.* Cambridge: Cambridge University Press: 298–388.

____. 1984. "The Southwest Midlands." In Thirsk (ed.), *The Agrarian History of England and Wales, 1640–1750, Vol I: Regional Farming Systems.* Cambridge, Cambridge University Press: 159–196.

Thornton, John. 1992. *Africa and Africans in the Making of the Atlantic World, 1400–1800.* Cambridge: Cambridge University Press.

Thornton, William Thomas. 1874 [1848]. *A Plea for Peasant Proprietors.* London: MacMillan and Co.

____. 1846. *Over-Population and Its Remedy.* London: Longman, Brown, Green and Longmans.

Thottathil, Sapna. 2012. "!ncredible Kerala?" PhD dissertation, UC Berkeley.

Times, 1860. Jan. 6.

____. 1844. June 14, 6.

____. 1844. June 11, 5.

____. 1844. June 10, 7.

____. 1844. June 7, 6.

____. 1844. March 23, 5, 6.

____. 1830."The Peasant's Friend," Nov. 6, 3.

____. 1830. Oct. 30, 3.

Tornquist, Ollie. 2000. "The New Popular Politics of Development: Kerala's Experience." In Govindan Parayil (ed.), *Kerala: The Development Experience. Reflections on Sustainability and Replicability.* London: Zed Press: 116–138.

Trollope, Anthony. 1859. *The West Indies and the Spanish Main.* London: Chapman & Hall.

Turner, M.E., J.V. Beckett, and B. Afton. 2001. *Farm Production in England, 1700–1914.* Oxford: Oxford University Press.

Underhill, Edward Bean. 1865. *A Letter Addressed to the Rt. Honourable E. Cardwell.* London: Arthur Miall.

United Nations Development Program. 2005. *Informe nacional de desarrollo humano.*

____. 2003. *Guatemala: una agenda para el desarrollo humano.*

Unni, Jeemol. 1983. "Changes in the Cropping Pattern in Kerala: Some Evidence on Substitution of Coconut for Rice, 1960–61 to 1978–79." *Economic and Political Weekly* 18, 39: 100–107.

USAID. 1975. *Small Farm Policy Analysis.* Washington DC.

Varghese, T.C. 1970. *Agrarian Change and Economic Consequences: Land Tenures in Kerala, 1850–1960.* Bombay: Allied Publishers.

Wade, Robert Hunter. 2001. "Making the World Development Report 2000:

Attacking Poverty." *World Development* 29, 8: 1435–1441.

Wagley, Charles. 1941. "Economics of a Guatemalan Village." *American Anthropological Association Memoir* 58.

Watts, Michael. 2013 [1983]. *Silent Violence: Food, Famine and Peasantry in Northern Nigeria.* Athens, Georgia: University of Georgia Press.

Wilken, Gene. 1987. *Good Farmers: Traditional Agricultural Resource Management in Mexico and Central America.* Berkeley: University of California Press.

Wilkinson, Daniel. 2002. *Silence on the Mountain: Stories of Terror, Betrayal, and Forgetting in Guatemala.* Boston: Houghton Mifflin.

Williams, James. 2001 [1837]. *A Narrative of Events since the First of August, 1834, by James Williams, an Apprenticed Labourer in Jamaica,* edited with an introduction by Diana Paton. Durham: Duke University Press.

Williams, Robert. 1994. *States and Social Evolution: Coffee and the Rise of National Governments in Central America.* Chapel Hill: University of North Carolina Press.

Winchilsea, Earl of. 1796. "On the Advantages of Cottagers Renting Land." *Annals of Agriculture, and Other Useful Arts* 26: 227–245.

Wise, Timothy. 2020. "Failing Africa's Farmers: An Impact Assessment of the Alliance for a Green Revolution in Africa." *Global Development and Environment Institute, Working Paper 20-01.* Tufts University (July).

Wittman, Hannah, Annette Aurélie Desmarais, and Nettie Wiebe (eds.). 2010. *Food Sovereignty: Reconnecting Food, Nature and Community.* Winnipeg: Fernwood Publishing.

Wolpert, Stanley. 2008. *A New History of India.* Oxford: Oxford University Press.

Woodward Jr., Ralph Lee. 1993. *Rafael Carrera and the Emergence of the Republic of Guatemala, 1821–1871.* Athens: University of Georgia Press.

World Bank. 2001. *World Development Report, 2000–2001: Attacking Poverty.* New York: Oxford University Press.

Wrigley, E.A. 2010. *Energy and the English Industrial Revolution.* Cambridge: Cambridge University Press.

____. 2004. *Continuity, Chance, Change: The Character of the Industrial Revolution in England.* Cambridge: Cambridge University Press.

Yadu, C.R. 2017. "Some Aspects of Agrarian Change in Kerala." *Journal of Land and Rural Studies* 5, 1 (January): 12–30.

Young, Arthur. 1950. *Travels in France During the Years 1787, 1788, and 1789,* ed. Constancia Maxwell. Cambridge: Cambridge University Press.

____. 1804. "On the Application of the Principle of Population to the Question of Assigning Land to Cottages." *Annals of Agriculture, and Other Useful Arts* 41: 208–231.

____. 1801. *An Inquiry into the Propriety of Applying Wastes for the Better Maintenance and Support of the Poor.* London: n.p.

____. 1801. "Cottager's Garden Calendar." *Annals of Agriculture, and Other Useful Arts* 36: 145–147.

____. 1791. "Memoirs of the Last Thirty Years of the Editor's Farming Life." *Annals of Agriculture, and Other Useful Arts* 15: 152–182.

Young, Crawford. 1994. *The African Colonial State in Comparative Perspective.* New Haven: Yale University Press.

Index

slavery, 78, 83
Ejectment Act, 41
Eliot, George, 123n
enclosure bills, 13
England
    agricultural inequality, 14
    beekeeping, 19
    Board of Agriculture and Internal
        Improvement, 16
    cottage gardens, 14
    crops, 19
    enclosure, 13-14, 16, 18
    livestock, 17
    peasant agriculture, 2, 11-12, 16-21
    poverty, 9, 11-15, 18
    unrest, 9, 24
    yeoman cavalry, 16
Eyre, Edward, 48

fertilizer, chemical, 112
Franke, Richard, 105
Fuentes, Miguel Ydígoras, 70
Fussell, G.E., 12

Gandhi, Indira, 111
genocide, 53-55
George, K.K., 106
Great Jamaican Rebellion of 1831, 37
Green Revolution, 110-111
    harms, 89
    India, 100, 111-114
    West Africa 88-90
Grey, Charles, 37
groundnuts, 85-86, 90, 93
Guatemala
    agriculture post-revolution, 65-66
    Campesino Unity Committee, 70-71
    coffee, 56-59
    cotton, 69
    crops, 53, 56, 63-64
    Decree 900, 66-68
    earthquake (1976), 70
    forced labour, 59-61
    land inequality, 65-67, 70
    livestock, 56, 63-64

peasant massacres, 71
peasant oppression, 68
US interference, 67-68
See also *milpa*

Hakewill, James, 34-35
Hall, Charles, 22
handicrafts, 91
Hardin, Garrett, 81
Hart, Keith, 87
Headey, Derek, 89
Heller, Patrick, 105
Homer-Dixon, Tad, 81-82
Hopkins, A.G., 91
Hyden, Goran, 87

India
    agrarian reform, 115
    coffee, 102
    crops, 104, 115
    green revolution, 100
    land inequality, 110, 115
    tea, 102
    pepper, 102, 113
industrial agriculture, 1-2, 5, 122
International Institute of Tropical
    Agriculture, 88

Jacob, T.G., 105
Jamaica
    coffee, 32
    cotton, 46
    corruption, 35
    crops, 31, 33, 43-44
    free villages, 42-3
    livestock, 35, 43, 47
    peasant agriculture, 31, 33
    provision grounds, 34, 40, 43
    slavery, 32-33, 37-41
    Sligoville, 41-42
    sugar, 32, 36-37, 45-47
Johnson, Lyndon, 111
Johnson, Michael, 89
Jones, Chester Lloyd, 61

Kaplan, Robert, 81-82

Acknowledgements

My comments are by necessity more limited than the debts I incurred in writing this book. I would first like to thank the Mayan farmers I have come to know in highland Guatemala. For over forty years they have impressed me with their knowledge and wisdom, inspired me with their hard work and astonished me with their resilience. They long ago taught me to appreciate the art of peasant livelihood.

My colleagues in the Department of History at the University of Saskatchewan have for over thirty years been generous and thoughtful. They make going to work each day a joy. This work was particularly inspired by a conversation with one of my colleagues, Geoff Cunfer. That we could in some ways disagree yet in cordial disagreement find inspiration is a testament both to his willingness to find value in others' ideas and to his amenable character. I wish also to thank Ben Hoy and the remarkable crew of students who work with him in the Historical Geographical Information Systems Lab for creating the maps for each of the chapters. Patrick Chassé provided invaluable research assistance for many of the chapters. I also relied on his excellent PhD dissertation for some of the evidence on Guatemala in Chapter 4.

The crew at Fernwood Publishing have been both efficient and a pleasure to work with. Thanks in particular to Jessica Herdman, Anumeha Gokhale, Jane Butler and Beverley Rach for their production and editing work, and to Annette Desmarais, Henry Veltmeyer and Raúl Delgado Wise, the series' editors. Errol Sharpe has been particularly supportive throughout.

I would like to thank especially Pedro Rafael González Chavajay, a most wonderful painter from San Pedro la Laguna in Guatemala, and the people at Artemaya for permission to use Pedro's painting on the cover.

As always, my most heartfelt thanks go to Annette.